TASTE

A LIFE IN WINE

TASTE

A LIFE IN WINE

Anthony Terlato

AGATE

CHICAGO

The recipes in this book are part of my collection of more than 400 recipes that we have enjoyed with our wines over the past 50 years. These original, modified, and (some) previously published recipes come from a variety of sources, including my grandmother's kitchen, highly acclaimed restaurants, noted chefs, and cookbooks dating back to 1899. Handed down through the years, the recipes as printed are how I prepare them in my home for family and friends. I gratefully acknowledge the many originators of these classic dishes.

Printed in the United States of America.

Trade paperback edition ISBN: 978-1-57284-106-2

The Library of Congress has cataloged the hardcover edition as follows:

Library of Congress Cataloging-in-Publication Data

Terlato, Anthony J., 1934-

Taste : a life in wine / Anthony J. Terlato.

    p. cm.

  Summary: "The autobiography of Anthony J. Terlato, chairman of the Terlato Wine Group"--Provided by publisher.

  ISBN-13: 978-1-57284-097-3 (hardcover)

  ISBN-10: 1-57284-097-8 (hardcover)

1. Terlato, Anthony J., 1934- 2. Vintners--California--Dry Creek Valley (Sonoma County)--Biography. 3. Viticulturists--California--Dry Creek Valley (Sonoma County)--Biography. 4. Wine and wine making--California--Dry Creek Valley (Sonoma County) 5. Wine industry--California--Dry Creek Valley (Sonoma County) 6. Terlato family. I. Title.

  TP547.T4A3 2008

  641.2'2092--dc22

  [B]

2008036391

10 9 8 7 6 5 4 3 2 1

Surrey Books is an imprint of Agate Publishing. Agate books are available in bulk at discount prices. For more information, go to agatepublishing.com.

Table of Contents

Foreword 7

Manhattan: November 6, 2006 15

Part I [1934–1956] 21

Brooklyn to Miami to Chicago 23

Leading Liquor Marts 39

Part II [1957–1978] 49

The Paterno Patrimony 51

Sicily: Land of Contrasts 69

Personally Selected By 79

The Right Time 89

Good Sports 109

Part III [1978–1981] 125

It's All in the Name 127

Casa Paterno, or Tony's Trattoria 169

Part IV [1982–2008] 185

California Revisited 187

Father and Sons 201

Old Stones and New Vines 221

Celebrations, Golden and Otherwise 241

Acknowledgments 261

Recipe Key 267

Foreword

ANTHONY J. TERLATO'S *TASTE: A LIFE IN WINE* IS NOT the usual CEO's narrative of climbing the corporate ladder from humble beginnings in Brooklyn to an impressive headquarters located in an exclusive suburb of Chicago. Nor is it simply a winemaker's tale of the pursuit of perfection in the glass. While Terlato's memoir incorporates both of these journeys, it also paints in broad strokes how one individual indefatigably worked to change America's wine-drinking habits from high alcohol to low, bulk rotgut to premium labels, and from sweet wine to dry. By doing so, he literally charted the course of this country's wine consumption, starting with the sweet and cheap Virginia Dare, Mogen David, and Central Valley Sauternes wines of the early 1950s and moving on to the inexpensive Portuguese rosés and jug wines of the 1960s, the very drinkable quality Italian wines of the early 1980s, and the premium boutique wines that the more knowledgeable and sophisticated public enjoys today.

In *Taste*, Terlato shares with his readers how his love for wine developed. He relates how he turned his father-in-law's import business into an extremely profitable high-end wine enterprise, and how he became the first salesman to invite wine professionals into his dining room, even constructing his own kitchen at the Pacific Wine Company to pair his wines with various foods that complemented them best. Later, he tells how he acquired vineyards in California and formed partnerships in wineries from France to Australia. Using good taste and ingenuity and always standing by his motto, "Quality Endures," Terlato read the past and anticipated the future of wine sales in America. As a result, he has lived a charmed life of fortuitous happenstance fueled by hard work.

But in this memoir, Terlato reveals more. He tells the story of post-Prohibition wine attitudes and sales in this country. During his first wine-related job—selling wines and spirits in his father's Chicago liquor supermarket—he discovered the French Grand Crus at a time when wine-industry legends Frank Schoonmaker and Alexis Lichine were making the case for French wine in the States. Within the two years following his marriage to Josephine (JoJo) Paterno, he moved on to selling San Joaquin Valley wines that his father-in-law, Anthony Paterno, bottled at the Pacific Wine Company and labeled with either a generic red wine label or the name of a local chain store. Domestic wines definitely had little appeal to a cocktail-drinking public, and Terlato's sales route took him to seedy liquor stores on Madison Street's Skid Row, where cheap, high-alcohol bottles were sold in brown paper bags to the city's down-and-outers. He threatened to quit, but ultimately he persuaded his father-in-law to consider bringing one or two of Lichine's selections into Chicago for him to sell. Within the next few years, Terlato visited Bordeaux and Burgundy, tasting and learning all the while. He and his father-in-law also traveled to Italy, bringing back contracts for quality Barolos, Bolla wines, and the Sicilian wine Corvo.

In the 1960s, the arc of Terlato's career coincided with Julia Child's rise to fame, and he shared her passion for French wines—if not for French food. Like her, but without the benefit of a TV platform, he placed a premium on awakening America's palate to good foods and good wines made with time-honored techniques and a tradition of gastronomic excellence. Through Pacific Wine's distributing business, his enthusiasm for Château Pétrus and Château Lafite echoed Child's much more public appreciation for a well-made *coulibiac de saumon* and *charlotte Malakoff au chocolat*. And in the 1970s, when he discovered the excellence of Italian wines and began importing them into the States, his childhood love of the simple dishes of Italy was reinforced by California's culinary focus on "fresh and seasonal" ingredients. Somehow, he always had his finger on the pulse of the nation's evolving gastronomy, from French to Italian, from California cuisine to regional fare, and eventually from ethnic dishes to fusion foods. His understanding of the various contemporary food trends resonated in his ever-growing portfolio of fine wines.

There are well-defined chapters in Terlato's evolving life story, and they all involve wine, food, and multiple examples of his instinctive entrepreneurial skills. The business acumen and vision evident in his latest ventures in winemaking were honed early on, when he began importing wines from Italy at a time when the term "Italian wine" meant nothing more to Americans than a straw-covered Chianti bottle paired with spaghetti and meatballs. In the 1960s and 1970s, he set out believing the best wines of Italy had not yet been discovered and exported to America, and he beat a path from the Piedmont region to Sicily to import the various quality wines that he found.

As a result of Terlato's focus on premium wines, the Chicago-based Pacific Wine Company experienced a period of dynamic expansion, distributing wines in quality liquor stores and wine shops. But very early on, Terlato also recognized that bringing his wines into restaurants would create a taste for them that would stimulate sales for home consumption and entertaining. So he concentrated his efforts on restaurant sales, an approach that was contrary to industry conventions. Appreciating and leveraging the link between fine wine and fine dining became one of Terlato's basic strategies. He went to high-end Michigan Avenue and Loop establishments, French and Italian restaurants, and even Chicago's pizza parlors, offering to train their waitstaff and print their wine lists if they would agree to include at least one of his brands.

Gradually, restaurant menus grew from offering little more than a choice of "a glass of red or a glass of white" to listing sparkling wines; imported Burgundies and Bordeaux; California's emerging brands, such as Charles Krug, Wente Brothers, and Louis Martini; and those quintessential favorites of the 1960s and 1970s —Lancers, Mateus, Bolla, and Blue Nun. In the 1980s, Terlato's quest for an Italian wine that would enhance an upscale Italian restaurant's offerings led him to discover Santa Margherita Pinot Grigio. Imports of the brand skyrocketed, boosted by his dynamic sales pitch and full-scale efforts. What had begun as a marketing strategy became an example of Terlato's prescience, and it exemplified his part in our country's growing appreciation of fine wines and gourmet foods during the second half of the 20th century.

His metamorphosis from a sales clerk in his father's liquor store to the United States' ultimate wine salesman is the narrative of his business dealings; along the way, he cultivated strong, long-lasting friendships with an impressive roster of major wine personalities, including Lichine, Schoonmaker, Angelo Gaja, Robert Mondavi, Christian Moueix, and Baroness Philippine de Rothschild. Many of his business associations, such as his importing agreement with Michel Chapoutier, have led to partnerships in winemaking in the United States, France, Italy, and Australia. His association with Rutherford Hill led directly to his purchase of the Napa winery in 1996 and his laser-like focus on producing exceptional wines.

For the past ten years, Terlato has given attention to every detail of his acquired vineyards. Sparing no expense in hiring winemakers and staff to experiment with the latest winemaking technology, he has set goals to attain the dream of a 90+ rating for his boutique wines. Time and time again, he has proven that he is committed to success and at the same time committed to quality—and he is willing to wait, in some cases as long as twenty-five years, to reel in a wine if necessary. But in his striving, he remains ever mindful of the hard work of his father and father-in-law, men who immigrated to this country and provided the opportunities to make his success possible. Likewise, he has brought his sons into the business to work with him—and eventually follow him.

As CEO and wine impresario of the Terlato Wine Group, Terlato shares insights and experiences that wine enthusiasts can only dream about—his 1956 honeymoon with his bride, JoJo, at the Charles Krug Winery in St. Helena at the invitation of proprietor Mondavi; ten years later, his accidental placement at a wine dinner in an empty chair next to Lichine that led to a contract and a longtime friendship; the warm and wonderful dinner party he hosted to celebrate his common birthday with Count Alexandre de Lur-Saluces of Château d'Yquem—of course, they saluted each other with a 1934 Yquem; and his discovery of barrels of Joe Rochioli's Pinot Noir while visiting the Williams Selyem winery. After tasting Rochioli's wine, he drove to the man's vineyard and walked away with a contract; a week later, Rochioli's Pinot Noir 1985 appeared on the cover of *Wine Spectator* as one of the three best California Pinot Noirs.

Unlike some wine professionals who concentrate on one area of the business—viticulture, enology, varietals, wine appreciation, food and wine pairings, and producers—Terlato knows the wine business inside out, including retail, bulk bottling, distributing, importing, marketing, sales, production, pairing wines with dishes, and even the importance of the aesthetics of a meal. From the simple pasta sauces he learned to make and serve to buyers at the Pacific Wine bottling company in Chicago in the late 1960s to the three-course lunches he takes pride in serving today at Tangley Oaks, the company's baronial headquarters, his choice of foods that showcase his wines is a vital part of his philosophy to educate both his employees and the public in the subtleties of wine.

Terlato also relates his many kitchen adventures when he cooked with award-winning chefs and winemakers. He adds memorable menus that pair his wines with recipes that were served at his homes in Napa, Palm Springs, Lake Geneva, and Lake Forest. And with his preference for the simple foods of the Italian table, he also shares traditional family recipes carefully devised with his chef at Tangley Oaks.

Told in his own words, Terlato's memoir is a progress report on the maturing of America's wine palate during the last half of the twentieth century and an insider's look into the wine trade. *Taste* is also a twenty-first century wine producer's odyssey.

—Joan Reardon
Lake Forest, Illinois
April 2008

Manhattan: November 6, 2006

WINE MAKES EVERY MEAL AN OCCASION, EVERY TABLE MORE ELEGANT, AND
EVERY DAY MORE CIVILIZED.

—*André Simon*

OUR PLANE LANDED AT TETERBORO AIRPORT AT
ten o'clock on a bright November morning. An hour later,
I stepped out of the car at the curb of the Time Warner
Center at Columbus Circle. My destination was Thomas Keller's
restaurant Per Se, where Terlato Wine Group's New York office had
organized a double-blind tasting of our latest releases alongside
other world-class wines for many of the top wine professionals in
New York. The event was sponsored by trusted business associate
and friend John Magliocco and his brother Nino, who owned
Peerless Distributors.

An elevator sped me to Per Se's private room for the tasting.
The Terlato wines that were to be tasted had been skillfully made
and carefully blended, so I knew they would perform well in
the tasting. My regional and district managers had taken care of
everything from the setup of the room to the temperature of the
wines. Usually, our tastings were for distributors; this one would
be for customers, including New York's most discriminating wine
managers, sommeliers, and restaurant owners. Some I knew, and
some I didn't, but John, his management team, and I quickly
engaged them in conversation.

I introduced the Terlato Wine Group by giving a short history of my life in the wine trade and an account of how our company has grown from a small distributorship to an importing business to winemaking. I was a Brooklyn-born kid who started out unpacking cases, putting up displays, and selling wine in his father's liquor store. Fifty years later, there I was, drinking the latest releases from my own vineyards.

I also told them that expanding my distributorships, bringing my two sons into the company, and developing a world-class portfolio had not changed my basic philosophy. If anything, acquiring vineyards in the Napa, Sonoma, and Santa Barbara regions and partnering in other winemaking ventures worldwide had only strengthened my resolve to link the Terlato name to quality.

Then, the double-blind tasting began. My staff had wrapped the six different wines—Terlato Vineyards Angels' Peak 2003, EPISODE by Terlato Vineyards 2002, Opus One 2002, Joseph Phelps Insignia 2002, Silver Oak 2002, and Dominus 2002—in paper bags to hide their identity. The thirty guests had forty-five minutes to taste the wines, summarize their thoughts, feelings, and opinions about each one, and select a favorite. I encouraged all the guests to take as much time as they needed to rate the wines in order of overall quality. A third party was engaged to tabulate the results, which I planned to announce during the luncheon that followed.

When the tasting was over, we poured the wonderful Italian sparkling wine Ca' del Bosco Brut for guests to enjoy during the short walk to Per Se's dining room. Best known for his sensational destination restaurant in the Napa Valley, the French Laundry, Thomas Keller went in a different direction for his return to New York City: The restaurant looks like a gilded corporate boardroom, with an elegant décor of modern brown tones, dark woods, and sleek metal surfaces. All sixteen of its well-spaced tables command a view of Central Park. As I escorted the guests to their tables, I felt confident about the setting and the menu, which had been carefully planned to showcase the wines by Per Se's chef de cuisine, Jonathon Benno.

After the first course of sea scallops, I spoke briefly about our long and productive relationship with Peerless Distributors and my personal friendship with John, and he returned the compliment in his remarks. As the luncheon's courses progressed from duck to prime rib, I revealed the results of the tasting.

To everyone's surprise—except mine—the Terlato wines received top scores.

I can only compare what I felt at that moment to other experiences that brought about the same rush of pride—the afternoon my son hit a home run, the day my granddaughter's excellent SAT scores arrived, and the moment *Wine Spectator* publisher Marvin Shanken called to tell me I'd received the magazine's Distinguished Service Award in 2004.

As I left the restaurant that afternoon, I tipped my hat eastward, across the East River to Brooklyn. That's where my story really begins, and I'm ready to tell it.

Peerless Importers Welcomes
Anthony Terlato
Featuring the Wines of
Terlato Vineyards

Menu
November 6, 2006
Per se
ten columbus circle, new york, new york 10019

Sautéed Maine Sea Scallops
Cauliflower Purée, Caramelized Cauliflower Florettes,
Lemon Confit, Croûtons de Brioche
and Brown Butter Emulsion

Terlato Vineyards, Pinot Grigio 2005

•

Aiguillette of Liberty Valley Pekin Duck Breast
Red Wine Poached Bartlett Pear, Glazed Tokyo Turnips, Mizuna Leaves
and Mignonnette de Foie Gras

Terlato Vineyards, Angels' Peak 2003

•

Herb Roasted Rib-Eye of Prime Beef
Rissolée of La Ratte Potatoes, Sweet Thumbelina Carrots,
Forest Mushrooms and Sauce Bordelaise

Domaine Terlato & Chapoutier, lieu dit Malakoff 2004

•

Pleasant Ridge Reserve
Michigan Sour Cherries, Black Pepper Shortbread,
Frisée Lettuce and Cherry Gastrique

EPISODE by Terlato Vineyards 2002

PART I

[1934—1956]

Brooklyn to Miami to Chicago

WHEN YOU'RE THE ONLY PEA IN THE POD, YOUR PARENTS ARE LIKELY TO
GET YOU CONFUSED WITH THE HOPE DIAMOND.

—Russell Baker

BROOKLYN! WHY HASN'T SOMEONE WRITTEN A blockbuster song about its trees, churches, homes, and bridges? Where else could anyone find the footprints of Herbie Mann, Bugsy Siegel, Mike Tyson, Barbara Stanwyck, and the Brooklyn Dodgers? Some of its monuments still stand, such as the Brooklyn Bridge and the Brooklyn Navy Yard, but others, like Ebbets Field, are long gone. Just the names of the neighborhoods are familiar around the country—Flatbush, Park Slope, Bay Ridge, Borough Park, Williamsburg, Gravesend, Clinton Hill, Crown Heights, Red Hook, and Bensonhurst—my neighborhood, the Italian community where I grew up.

At the time I was born, on May 11, 1934, my mother, father, and maternal grandmother lived together in a single-family house on West 6th Street and Avenue T. Back then, the neighborhood was not heavily Italian. My father was born in Italy and came to America at the age of four, in 1908. He was fluent in Italian, academically gifted, and eventually entered law school. Unfortunately, during the Depression, he was forced to leave law school and settle into a career in insurance and real estate.

The year before the United States entered World War II, my family moved to Bensonhurst. During the war, things changed dramatically. Manhattan's skyline was darkened every night to thwart air attacks from the enemy and prevent German U-boats from sighting American vessels in the ports and harbor. Even the Statue of Liberty's torch was extinguished, and the observation decks on the tallest buildings were closed. For a grammar-school kid peering across the river at the big city, it was a heady time.

I listened to my parents, did what was right, and thought that was how the whole world lived. I had a good family life. I was very happy, and we never knew poverty. We were just like all the other families around us. There were probably challenges that I had to overcome, but I didn't really notice them.

My family always had a jug of wine cooling in the hallway. At every evening meal, my father would pour glasses for himself, my mother, and my grandmother, and he would always mix a small amount with water for me. As far back as I can remember, I was taught that food and wine went together and that special wines were served with special dishes on special occasions, such as weddings and holidays.

My strongest Italian connection came from my Nonna, Giuseppina Giarrusso, who had immigrated to the United States from Sicily in 1910 and worked alongside my grandfather Giovanni in his butcher shop. After my grandfather's death in 1931, Nonna moved in with my parents. She remained an integral part of our family until her death in 1969.

Nonna was a terrific cook, but I never saw her use a recipe. She prepared simple and delicious Italian food for almost every meal we ate. Every morning as I left the house for school, she would ask, "*Cosa posso cucinare per te stasera, principe mio?*" ("What can I cook for you this evening, my prince?") To this day, I vividly remember the aroma of one of my favorite dishes—veal cutlet,

Melrose peppers, and tomato sauce—simmering on the stove when I walked through the door. I honestly believed that no other kid in all of Bensonhurst ate such delicious meals.

Most of my early memories are of the meals my extended family shared together. All our holidays and weddings were true celebrations, with traditional foods and marvelous wines. In one photo taken at a family wedding when I was twelve, I'm pictured drinking a glass of red wine and showing off a brand-new suit.

I was an only child. Let's face it: I was the center of attention. During my early years, I took everything for granted and never questioned any of it. It wasn't until much later in life that I realized I usually behaved more like an adult than a child because most of my interactions were with adults. I never knew what it was like to have a brother or sister. I was comfortable with adults, mostly because my parents taught me how to behave myself.

I imitated everything my father did. One day after my father had gone to work, I tried to shave with his Gillette razor and ended up shaving some of my hair off. (That earned me a good spanking from my mother.) My father brushed and polished his shoes regularly, and so did I. I also shared my father's passion for opera. Whenever he was home, there was music playing in our house, and I could whistle "La donna è mobile" from *Rigoletto* by the time I was ten. To this day, I like nothing better than a Puccini or Verdi opera.

My father's parents, Anthony and Catherine Terlato, also lived in Brooklyn, but every April through September they ran an upstate inn called Terlato's Vacation Land in Clintondale, New York. Vacation Land was a hundred-acre farm with an apple orchard, hundreds of blueberry and raspberry bushes, a tennis court, a candy store, and a small soda fountain, where I enjoyed many ice cream sodas.

Every summer, my mother and I spent a month at the inn at the peak of the season. When my father came up on weekends, he would join us in the kitchen—even spit-roasting a pig on occasion. My days at Vacation Land were filled with horse rides at the stables across the street, target practice with my trusty Red Ryder BB gun, and fruitful forays into the apple orchard and strawberry patches with my grandfather.

The house could accommodate at least ten couples, which meant there was plenty of room for us. Grandmother Terlato served wonderful meals boarding-house style, and every evening's menu was different. At the big dining room table, guests passed around large platters of pasta and sausage, sautéed spinach, roast chicken, and grilled steaks, all made fresh each day. After dinner, everyone would gather in the living room with guitars, banjos, and mandolins and sing songs like "Amapola" and the "Ferryboat Serenade."

Throughout my childhood, I watched my father, a gentle and patient man, work very hard selling insurance and real estate. He was a good-looking man—trim, stylish, and well dressed, almost always wearing a starched shirt, perfectly knotted tie, and spotless shoes. He never cursed in our house or anywhere else in front of my mother—to do so was unthinkable.

My mother, a strong, no-nonsense woman, was slender and pretty, the kind of woman who went to the beauty parlor to have her hair set and nails manicured because it proved to family, friends, and neighbors that her husband could afford a few luxuries. She kept up the house and kept a short leash on me, making sure that I delivered the papers on my route on time and was polite when I delivered groceries for the owner of the local corner store. Like many women of the time, she was family oriented, but she also contributed to the family's income without leaving home by doing intricate embroidery on coats made at a nearby factory.

My Nonna, who was very refined and attractive, never remarried after her husband died. Whenever anyone asked why she'd never considered it, she'd tell them, "I've already had the best, and there's no need to look. No one could take his place."

Even though my mother and father were both only children, just like me, I had many relatives who spoiled me. Vita, one of my favorite relatives from New Jersey, visited Manhattan every year with her husband, Tony. They always took to the Paramount Theatre for action movies and live performances by acts like Louis Prima and Abbott and Costello, or the Roxy for a play or a vaudeville show. After the show, we'd all head to Chinatown for dinner.

As I progressed from grammar school at St. Athanasius to high school at Brooklyn Preparatory, my father dreamed that I would become a lawyer or doctor. My brief stint as an altar boy led my mother and grandmother to dream that I'd join the priesthood. None of these options was for me.

I got decent grades, but I really didn't like much about school except history and sports. I excelled at baseball and basketball throughout my academic career. In retrospect, I suppose that I considered every game a battle that was to be won at any cost.

Perhaps not surprisingly, the teachers I admired most were also coaches. In high school, Father Anthony Paone was one of the few Italian priests who taught us, and he became a mentor to me and the other two Italian kids in our class. He looked after us and pushed us to do better. He had once been a boxer, and on one occasion, I got a little too wise with him, provoking him to say, "Why don't we get in the ring? I'd like to teach you a little bit about boxing." I thought for a moment, considered the potential for injury, and replied, "Tell me what you want me to do better instead." Father Paone had my number and never missed an opportunity to take me down a peg or two when I needed it. Eventually, I earned his respect, and we became great friends.

One of my math teachers, A. Martin Stader, had been a weight lifter and a football player, so his punishments tended toward the physical. If he caught someone talking in class, for example, he'd order the offender to hold his algebra or geometry book over his head for the rest of the class. By the time the bell rang, the book felt like it weighed a thousand pounds. Stader really kept everyone in line, and I respected him.

I hung out with a pretty big group of boys after school and on weekends. Our days were filled with baseball, basketball at the Y, swimming at Coney Island, and, of course, flirting with girls at the local outdoor pool. We didn't have much time or reason to pick on other kids, particularly because we didn't want to disappoint our parents.

The first car I bought was a 1939 black Chevrolet stick shift, for $50. I polished it up, put on whitewall tires, drove it for a year, and sold it for $75. For my eighteenth birthday, my Nonna bought me a tan 1946 Ford convertible so I could drive to school in style.

———————

After high school, my father persuaded me to pursue a degree in business administration at his alma mater, Brooklyn's St. Francis College. During my second year, however, I decided to leave; I really wanted to be a part of the business world, and at that point, I felt that I was only marking time in college. I took an entry-level job at the Savings Bank of Brooklyn, and even though I made only $40 a week, my mother was proud to tell her friends her son worked at the bank.

One day, the bank's vice president of new accounts asked if I would drop him off at his house. As I drove, we began to chat about the banking business. He told me that I was a quick study and that I could look forward to a bright future at the bank. When we reached his house, he said, "Wait out here for a minute. I want to show you something."

He opened his garage door, revealing a new green Chevrolet parked inside.

"It's my first new car," he said with pride.

"Congratulations! Have a nice evening." I returned to my car and drove away. He had been working at the bank for twenty years! I asked myself, "What the hell am I doing? Do I want to wait twenty years to buy a new car?" Banking was not for me. It was all politics, with people maneuvering over where they sat, where they ate lunch, and who they befriended. Working at a bank was not for me—unless I owned it.

A few weeks later, I told my father, "I don't like this bank stuff. I'm quitting and going to Florida to start something of my own." He asked me what I planned to do there, and I had to answer, "I have no idea, but Miami Beach is where I want to go." To be honest, the only reason I could come up with was that it was much warmer than Brooklyn.

———————

My friend Herb Bogart joined me on my adventure. We packed our bags, loaded my car, and took off for Florida. When we arrived, our first stop was an employment agency. A woman at the agency told us about openings for three bellboys at the Broadripple Hotel, which was right across the street from the Sorrento and Sovereign hotels and adjacent to the site where the Fontainebleau Hotel was under construction.

Without blinking an eye, I told the woman, "We'll take them." She repeated that the Broadripple was looking for three bellboys.

I answered, "What are the shifts? We'll do them all. We'll do the whole twenty-four hours between us."

She said, "That's impossible! That's twelve hours apiece."

But we did it. We worked around the clock, earning a few bucks here and there for carrying bags and delivering suntan lotion, newspapers, and drinks.

At the same time, we kept our living expenses as low as possible. At first, we rented a small apartment in an area where most of the residents were fellow hotel employees. We figured that because of our work schedules, only one of us would be in the apartment at any given time. Since the rent was based on the number of occupants in the apartment, I told the manager that only I would be living there. Herb and I were pretty similar looking, but eventually we were found out—and kicked out.

Working in Miami really meant living on a tight budget, so I was thrilled to find Lou Paoletti's restaurant on Biscayne Boulevard. The pizza was delicious and very inexpensive, so I ate there almost every night. Eventually Lou realized that I had very little money, so every once in a while, he would send out a dish and say, "This is a new recipe I'm trying. What do you think of it?" It was his gracious way of giving me a free hot meal without embarrassing me. In return, I sent many hotel guests there, telling them it was the best Italian restaurant in Miami Beach. Even after I began making more money, I still ate at Paoletti's three times a week.

After a while, my friend gave up on Miami Beach and went home to Brooklyn. My fortunes in Miami Beach were on the upswing: I took a doorman position and a car-parking concession at the Sovereign Hotel. There, I was the boss—I was in charge of the valets, and I split tips with the runners who parked the cars. If a guest's car needed an oil change, I'd arrange it. If a guest wanted to go to a show, I knew who to call for tickets. If a guest wanted to spend an afternoon at the track, I'd arrange a limousine and a box for him. In no time at all, I was making more than $300 a week—a lot better than the $40 I had been making at the bank. I had Miami—even top hotels like the Saxony and the Sans Souci— all figured out.

Once the Fontainebleau opened, things got even better. The hotel's pool was its crown jewel, and I was a strong swimmer. I befriended the guy who was in charge of the Fontainebleau's sports activities and let him know that I'd like to work there as a swimming and diving instructor. I was only an adequate diver, but I was very good at teaching kids how to swim.

After only two years in Miami Beach, I locked up the concessions for swimming lessons, towels, and suntan lotion at the Fontainebleau and two hotel car-parking concessions. I knew the concierges at most of the big hotels on Miami Beach, and they called me when guests wanted tickets to see Judy Garland, Frank Sinatra, Dean Martin, and all the other stars that the Fontainebleau attracted. I was only twenty-one years old, but I knew without a doubt that I would always find a way to succeed.

I was also very single. I could go out with a different good-looking girl every night in Miami Beach. It was like being a kid in a candy store. I always knew where the hottest acts were appearing, and there was always a party somewhere to crash.

I carefully watched the patrons of the hotel. I depended on tips to pay my bills. There are people who tip well and people who don't, and I quickly learned how to differentiate those who tipped from those who didn't. Some guests would say, "I'll take care of you when I leave," and never did, and others would tell me, "I'd like to have my beach chair over on this side of the pool every morning," and then slip me a tip each time. Good tippers walk, talk, and look a certain way, and it was up to me to tell the difference. I gave the best service to guests who I thought would reward me for it. Sometimes I made mistakes, but I learned from them. This talent of sizing up people has served me well in business.

Back home in Brooklyn, my father retired from the real estate business and decided to open a liquor store near our home. Unfortunately, he faced tight restrictions on liquor licenses there. Licensing laws gave priority to Korean War veterans' applications, and a veteran had already applied for a license across the street from the site my father had selected. At the time, liquor stores in Brooklyn had to be at least one mile apart, so my father was forced to look elsewhere.

At that point, fate intervened. My father and mother joined two of their cousins on a cruise to Italy, and on board my father ran into an old friend, Anthony Paterno, who owned the Pacific Wine Company in Chicago. Like many other Italians, Paterno had moved from Brooklyn to Chicago, opened a grocery store, and bought into a wine-bottling business. My father told Paterno of his thwarted plans to open a liquor store in Brooklyn, and Paterno replied, "Why not come to Chicago? You can open a liquor store anywhere you want. I'll help you." The seed was planted.

After my parents returned from Italy, my father called and asked me to come home to help them celebrate their twenty-fifth wedding anniversary. Even at the time, I knew it was a ploy, but I really wanted to be with my family again—especially my grandmother.

Sure enough, after my arrival, my father told me about his plans to go to Chicago and embark on his new career in the retail liquor business. My uncle planned to join my father in the business, and they wanted me to be a part of their new endeavor. I was very sure that my future lay in Miami, but I agreed to join my father in Chicago for a month—just to help him start up the business. Afterward, I'd be back in Miami, where the sky was the limit.

Nonna Giarrusso's Veal and Melrose Peppers

In Brooklyn, Nonna Giarrusso used small green bell peppers to make this dish, but when we all moved to Chicago in 1955, she found a pepper that was widely used by the Italian community in the western suburb of Melrose Park. Smaller, elongated, thinner skinned, and less fleshy than a bell pepper, the Melrose pepper added just the right amount of flavor and texture to the dish as it counterpointed the tomato sauce.

SERVES 6

5 to 7 tablespoons olive oil, divided

1 small onion, sliced

1 large clove garlic, bruised

2 cans (28 ounces each) Italian plum tomatoes

6 large basil leaves, cut into ribbons

Salt and pepper, to taste

20 Melrose peppers (or small green peppers), tops removed and seeded

1 cup grated Parmigiano-Reggiano cheese

2 pounds veal cut into 24 scaloppine (thin slices) or cutlets

1. To prepare tomato sauce: Heat 2 tablespoons olive oil over medium heat in large saucepan. Add onion and garlic; cook and stir until onion is soft. Remove garlic. Add tomatoes and basil; simmer for 15 minutes, stirring occasionally. Season with salt and pepper to taste. Set aside.

2. Heat 2 tablespoons olive oil in large skillet over medium heat until hot. Cook peppers in hot oil until skin turns golden brown and starts to bubble on both sides. Season with salt and pepper. Remove from skillet and set aside.

3. Heat 1 tablespoon olive oil in same large skillet over medium heat; do not let oil smoke. Quickly cook each slice of veal in hot oil (about 30 to 40 seconds per side), adding more oil as needed. Season to taste. Remove from skillet and set aside.

4. To assemble: Place 12 slices of sautéed veal in bottom of large baking pan. Top each slice with a pepper, a large spoonful of tomato sauce and 1 teaspoon Parmigiano-Reggiano cheese. Repeat layers. Serve at room temperature with crusty Italian bread.

SUGGESTED WINES

Rutherford Hill Merlot, Markham Cabernet Sauvignon

CHICKEN ALLA MILANESE

"Alla Milanese" signifies nothing more precise than breaded cutlets of meat, especially veal, sautéed in butter. We used chicken and loved the combination of arugula and either cherry or grape tomatoes in a bit of olive oil when these items were available in the local farmers' markets.

SERVES 4

4 chicken breast halves, skinned and boned

2 large eggs

1 ½ cups bread crumbs

2 teaspoons fresh or dried oregano, chopped

2 cloves garlic, minced

1 teaspoon kosher salt

1 teaspoon fresh black pepper

4 tablespoons parsley, chopped and divided

4 tablespoons olive oil, divided

2 tablespoons lemon juice

2 cups baby arugula leaves

10 cherry tomatoes, cut in half

1. Flatten the chicken breasts to ½-inch thickness by pounding between two sheets of plastic wrap.

2. In a medium bowl, whisk eggs.

3. On a plate, mix bread crumbs with oregano, garlic, salt, pepper, and 2 tablespoons parsley.

4. Dip chicken in beaten eggs, turn to coat and then dredge in the bread crumb mixture, coating completely.

5. Heat 3 tablespoons olive oil in a large skillet over medium heat.

6. Add chicken and sauté until golden brown and cooked, about 5 minutes per side. Transfer chicken to plates.

7. In a medium bowl, toss arugula and cherry tomatoes with remaining oil. Sprinkle with salt and pepper and a dash of lemon juice.

8. Sprinkle chicken with the lemon juice and remaining 2 tablespoons parsley and place the seasoned arugula and cherry tomatoes over the chicken in a mound or on the side.

SUGGESTED WINES
Sanford Pinot Noir, Terlato Family Vineyards Chardonnay

Leading Liquor Marts

WHEN I WAS TWENTY-ONE, IT WAS A VERY GOOD YEAR...

—Ervin Drake

AFTER BROOKLYN AND MIAMI, CHICAGO WAS A WHOLE new ballgame. The drive up Lake Shore Drive from the South Shore Country Club to the North Shore suburb of Evanston was one of the most beautiful rides I'd ever taken. Frank Sinatra had it right—"You lose your blues in Chicago" and jump right into a great jazz scene. You can walk along State Street, "that great street," and gawk your way along the Magnificent Mile from the Wrigley Building to the Drake Hotel.

From the moment my father, uncle, and I arrived in Chicago, Anthony Paterno treated us like family. Paterno was an incredibly generous, big-hearted man who was completely devoted to his wife, Lena. Likewise, Lena's hospitality was legendary; she would extend the family meal to accommodate any number of guests at a moment's notice. I remember sitting around their dining room table the first evening we were in town—June 10, 1955. That night was special, because it was his daughter Josephine's (nicknamed JoJo) twenty-first birthday.

I liked JoJo immediately. She was about five foot two, with beautiful dark hair. She was a smart dresser and a terrific dancer. That evening at dinner, I found out how intelligent she was, and I admired how hard she worked in her father's business. As JoJo blew out the candles on her birthday cake that night, I looked into her sparkling eyes. Little did I know that my fate was sealed.

Paterno's son, John, was also at the dinner, along with his wife, Antonette. I liked John immediately; he was a warm and wonderful person. Also in attendance at the celebration was Paterno's youngest daughter, Michelin, who was still in grammar school. We all celebrated and toasted the future—including our family's new venture.

———————

There were only a few wine shops in Chicago in the 1950s, but there were plenty of corner taverns and small shops that sold liquor from behind the counter. At the time, there was only one real self-serve, supermarket-style liquor store in the city—Armanetti Liquors. My father's store became the second. He leased a former Jewel supermarket space on the north side of the city, at the intersection of Clark Street and Ridge Avenue. It was a strategically important location because it was only about three miles from the Chicago/Evanston border—and Evanston, the birthplace of the Women's Christian Temperance Union, was as dry as the desert. The store was also in a heavy traffic area, not far from the fine residences of Lake Shore Drive, the Edgewater Beach Hotel, Edgewater Hospital, and Loyola University. My father hoped to appeal to a discriminating clientele of city dwellers as well as the suburban crowd heading for Evanston and beyond.

In the mid-1950s, only a few upper-class restaurants featured wine. The wine list of Kungsholm Restaurant, which was located on Rush Street in the former Cyrus McCormick Mansion, included Mumm's Champagne for $14 a bottle, the American sparkling wine Cook's for $6, some French Burgundies and Sauternes, Gold Seal American Burgundies, and a German Liebfraumilch. Market surveys of the time found that ninety percent of the American public didn't think table wine was a drink for ordinary people; instead, they thought it was only for the rich, foreigners, and immigrants. However, middle-class Americans were making a beeline for the growing number of inexpensive fast-food restaurants, such as McDonald's and Kentucky Fried Chicken, that began to dot the landscape, and they were slowly warming to the appearance of Gallo's first pop wines, Thunderbird and Ripple, and Cold Duck for special occasions.

Wine had always been on the dining tables of recent immigrants from Mediterranean countries (like my own family), but until the 1960s, quality wines were mostly consumed by the wealthy and well traveled. Tea was the drink of choice with meals, and coffee was a close second. Sweet wines were the province of ladies, consumed as aperitifs or digestives. Selling table wine to the average American was an uphill battle, so my father had his work cut out for him.

Anthony Paterno helped us every inch of the way. He recommended people to install fixtures in the store, provided wholesaler contacts, and hosted us for dinner two or three nights a week, but still we all missed Nonna's cooking (my mother and grandmother were still in Brooklyn).

My father renovated the store, installed shelves and racks for wine, purchased a walk-in refrigerator, and decorated the walls with trellises and artificial grapes. He christened it Leading Liquor Marts, and a few short months later, on September 1, 1955, we opened for business.

I was caught up in the excitement of the store, and summer was bringing the city of Chicago to life. I was also feeling a gravitational pull toward a very lovely young lady. Miami Beach was looking less and less attractive.

After the store opened, my mother and grandmother joined

us in Chicago, and the store became a real family enterprise. My father, uncle, and I worked from nine in the morning until the store closed at ten in the evening. My mother worked one of the cash registers, and my grandmother used the service kitchen to prepare lunch and dinner every day for the family. Invariably, we ate on the run, and sometimes we were too busy to eat at all.

From the very beginning, my father's focus was on quality. Leading Liquor Marts sold seventy-seven brands of imported beers at a time when Schlitz was overwhelmingly Chicago's beer of choice. He stocked quality brands of single-malt Scotches and single-batch bourbons. One ninety-foot-long wall featured racks and racks of the world's finest wines—Burgundies, Bordeaux, you name it. Customers strolled up and down the aisles, picking up bottles and reading the labels in a leisurely way.

I fell in love with my father's supermarket concept. Beer and gin were part of our business, and vodka was just about to be discovered, but the part of the business that fascinated me was the wine section. We often opened a few wines for customers to taste, and invariably what they tasted would end up in their carts. We opened a bottle for tasting for any customer who expressed interest in buying a case.

Most wine stores of the time offered little more than Virginia Dare, a wine made from Scuppernong grapes and sold in maple syrup–style bottles; sweet Central Valley Sauterne, Sherry, Port, and Muscatel sold by the gallon jug; and a few kosher wines, such as Mogen David. My father stocked a wide range of classic Bordeaux and Burgundy vintages, including '45, '47, '49, and '53. It's incredible to imagine it now, but he sold Château Lafite, Latour, and Margaux for $3.98 a bottle. In the 1950s, it didn't cost much to drink absolutely wonderful wines. I quickly learned that the best customers—the businessmen who lived on or near

Lake Shore Drive, the professors from Loyola University, and the doctors who practiced at Edgewater Hospital—had acquired a taste for better wines either during a time in service overseas or because their business had taken them to explore postwar Europe.

I always preferred to work the wine side of the store, and I quickly realized that the people who were buying the better wines were the people I really enjoyed helping. A customer might say, "I really enjoyed the wine you recommended last time. Tomorrow, I have friends coming over and I'm grilling steaks. What wine would you recommend?" That kind of repeat customer made my day.

My passion and love for wine began right there in the aisles of Leading Liquor Marts. I read every book that I could find about wine and bought magazines like *The New Yorker* and *Gourmet* to discover what wine experts like Alexis Lichine and Frank Schoonmaker had to say about French wines and fine dining. I read until I knew which wines were important, where they came from, and what they should taste like. Next, I tasted almost all the wines on that ninety-foot wall, two at a time, with paper bags over the bottles. I learned to taste the difference between Cabernet Sauvignon and Pinot Noir, between Chardonnay and Riesling.

Working the retail channel of the business also taught me to work harder than my competitors. Once, we advertised a carton of cigarettes for $1.99 and a bottle of Canadian Club whisky for $3.99 as "loss leaders," a common tactic to bring shoppers into the store. (The cigarettes cost us $2 and the Canadian Club $4, so we lost a penny on every sale.) It brought in the customers, all right, but not always in the way that we had hoped.

I told my father, "It's hard to say, 'Thank you very much and come back soon' to these customers. Think about it. Too many people are coming in here just to buy the loss leaders in the window." We switched gears and rearranged the store, putting the most profitable items in the front of the store, where customers would see our better stock right away. Why feature Corby's Whiskey for $2.79 when we could sell Seagram's 7 at $4.29—a healthy profit? Why shouldn't the customer pass a shelf of seven $4.99 Scotches before finding Black & White for $3.99? Why put a $2 bottle of wine at a customer's fingertips when he had $5 to spend?

What little spare time I had away from the store was spent getting to know Chicago. It wasn't the most subtle move, but I asked JoJo to show me the sights, and she agreed. JoJo and I saw *La Boheme* at the Lyric Opera and afterward strolled a few blocks down to the London House to enjoy a few drinks and hear the smooth jazz piano of Ramsey Lewis. We often visited Rush Street, just north of the Loop, for its hodgepodge of movie houses, bars, and trendy restaurants like Mr. Kelly's.

Back in Brooklyn, I'd brought a few girls home to meet my family, and, well, my grandmother didn't like most of them. One girl I'd dated in Florida called the house looking for me, and my grandmother told her I had moved away—to Australia! But with JoJo, it was different. Nonna loved JoJo right away. She was what my grandmother called a "good girl." Nonna told me I shouldn't go back to Florida. Instead, she told me, I should marry JoJo.

During the summer months, before the store had opened, JoJo and I saw the Cubs play at Wrigley Field and hit the beaches of Lake Michigan. In the fall, we went to football games at Northwestern University's Dyche Stadium, and over the winter, we celebrated the holidays with both of our families. The more I got to know JoJo, the better I understood that my grandmother was right! JoJo and I became inseparable.

Nonna gave me a thousand dollars—a huge amount of money

at that time—to buy her an engagement ring. She cautioned, "Buy a gem," and I understood what she meant. She wanted me to buy a quality diamond, not one that was ostentatious and flawed. I bought a flawless stone that JoJo still treasures today.

JoJo and I were married on April 21, 1956. She was resplendent in a Juliet cap, lace veil, and long satin wedding gown. The wedding was held at the Sherman House in Chicago, and my father-in-law invited all of his friends and business associates, along with his and my family. We celebrated our marriage with more than 1,200 guests that evening. The grand ballroom was lined with buffet tables overflowing with food, and the waiters poured Mirafiore Asti Spumante all night long. Half of the evening was over before we finally ended the receiving line and danced our first dance.

To be sure, 1956 was a very good year.

CANNOLI

Imported from Sicily, these ricotta-filled fried-dough shells have always been a traditional accompaniment to special occasions. They were served at our wedding along with Mirafiore Asti Spumante, and through the years, JoJo has perfected the recipe.

SERVES 6

Shells:

1 cup sifted flour

1½ tablespoons butter

¼ teaspoon salt

3 teaspoons sifted confectioner's sugar

1 egg beaten with 1 tablespoon Marsala wine

1 egg white, lightly beaten with 1 teaspoon water

3 cups vegetable oil for frying

1½ cups ricotta filling

1. Sift all dry ingredients into a mixing bowl; cut in butter with a pastry blender or in a processor.

2. Add egg mixture and pulse until dough sticks together. Knead into a ball, wrap in plastic wrap and refrigerate at least 30 minutes.

3. To make the cannoli shells, divide the dough in half. On a floured surface, roll out the dough into a strip about 16 × 5½ × ⅛ inch thick. Using a 4-inch round cutter, cut out dough and roll into ovals about 5 × 3½ inches. Place a cannoli tube down the length of the oval, bring the sides up and over and seal the dough with egg wash.

4. Heat the oil in a deep fryer to 365°F. Fry the cannoli a few at a

time until golden. Remove with a tong and drain on absorbent paper. When the shells are still warm to the touch, remove the tubes by holding one end of the tube with a pot holder and gently easing the shell off the tube by hand using absorbent paper for protection. Cool shells completely.

5. Before serving, fill the cannoli shells, using a pastry bag fitted with a large plain tip. If desired, dip both ends in pistachio nuts.

Ricotta Filling:

2 cups whole milk ricotta or 1½ cup ricotta and ½ cup goat cheese

⅔ cup sugar

1 teaspoon vanilla extract or orange essence

¼ teaspoon salt

Slivered candied orange peel (optional)

Finely chopped pistachio nuts (optional)

1. Spoon the ricotta into a strainer lined with cheesecloth. Set over a bowl and drain overnight in the refrigerator.

2. Process the cheese in a processor to lighten it; add the sugar, vanilla, salt, and orange peel if desired. Refrigerate until ready to use.

Suggested Wines

Santa Margherita Prosecco, Chapoutier Banyuls, Peller Estates Vidal Blanc

PART II

[1957—1978]

The Paterno Patrimony

PEOPLE THINK I'M DISCIPLINED. IT IS NOT DISCIPLINE. IT IS DEVOTION.
THERE IS A GREAT DIFFERENCE.

—*Luciano Pavarotti*

JOJO AND I HONEYMOONED IN SAN FRANCISCO, JUST A stone's throw away from the Napa Valley, the epicenter of winemaking in North America. The Mondavi brothers, Peter and Robert (Bob), had made quite a name for their family business, the Charles Krug Winery. Peter was the winemaker, and Bob was the marketing dynamo. By the mid-1950s, Krug, Beaulieu, Inglenook, Louis Martini, and Beringer were the "Big Five" wine producers in the Napa Valley.

My father-in-law and Bob and Peter's father, Cesare Mondavi, had been friends and business associates for years, with a relationship that started when Paterno began selling Mondavi's Zinfandel and Muscat grapes to Chicago families who made their own wine at home. When Mondavi bought Charles Krug Winery, my father-in-law became his Illinois distributor. So when Bob heard that JoJo and I would be honeymooning in San Francisco, he suggested that we spend some time in the Napa Valley with him and his first wife, Marjorie.

At the time, the Napa Valley town of St. Helena was little more than a main drag with a bakery, a drug store, a butcher shop, a hardware store, an automobile showroom, the local newspaper, and our honeymoon hideaway, the El Bonita Motel. Our destination, the Charles Krug Winery, was located just north of town. Early every morning, around seven o'clock, I joined Bob at the winery to taste his wines and discuss his marketing strategies.

I was amazed to learn about his relationships with restaurateurs. He traveled to San Francisco to sell his wines to the city's finest restaurants. Once the restaurant agreed to sell the wine, he would offer to make up a wine list to include in the menus, and Mondavi's assistant, Larry Romano, would brief the restaurant's waiters about the wines. He explained the wine's history in great detail, including information about the terrain where the grapes were grown and the proper foods to match with the various types of wine. He held tastings for the staff, so all of them knew firsthand what the wines tasted like. Mondavi also taught the staff how to properly open a bottle of wine—how to remove the cork, how to hold the bottle, how to pour the first glass, and how to wait for the customer to taste it.

When restaurant patrons requested a wine list, the Mondavi-coached waiters would share the Krug wines' history with them. Nobody else was doing this in 1956—especially in Chicago. Mondavi's brilliant plan inspired me. I decided to tell my father-in-law about his technique, so he could replicate the approach in Chicago. He could sell wine to restaurants and conduct waitstaff training sessions, just as Robert had done.

After I'd spent a good part of each day with Bob, JoJo and I would spend some time in town and then prepare for dinner at the Mondavi home on the vineyard property. Every evening, we enjoyed Marjorie's cooking, Bob's wines, and their hospitality. I immediately identified with Bob's passion for wine and his zest for business. Even though he was twenty-one years my senior, our relationship quickly developed. Bob Mondavi became my friend as well as my mentor.

When I returned to Chicago, I set up a small tasting table in my father's store. Each Saturday and Sunday, I opened two white and two red wines for customers to taste and compare. The customers learned, and I did as well. I tasted at least four new wines a week at the store in addition to what I took home each night.

Before JoJo and I went to Napa, I'd already been bitten by the wine bug. I knew it was an opportunity to be on the ground floor of what I felt was an emerging business. After our trip, however, I became convinced that my future was in wine. I had countless ideas—opening another store that sold wine only, for one—and I couldn't wait for that future to begin.

Upon our return to Chicago, JoJo and I settled into our own apartment, a third-floor walk-up. (I really disliked carrying groceries up those three flights of stairs.) JoJo continued to work for her father as secretary and bookkeeper at the Pacific Wine Company, and I continued to work in my father's store. Now, I had more enthusiasm to learn about wine than ever before. My father and I hired a few clerks at the retail store, so we were able to live a more normal life than we had in the past year. We still worked seven days a week, but at least we could alternate working days and nights and Sundays.

At the end of each day's work, I would call JoJo to find out what she was preparing for dinner. I would select two bottles of wine—one ordinary and one from a high-quality winery—to bring home to taste. JoJo would pour two glasses of each wine for me and for herself, without telling me which was which, and we'd drink the wines with our meal. After a year or so of these informal blind tastings with JoJo over dinner, I began to understand the difference between the wines. I could recognize the perfume, the color, the taste, and the aftertaste of each wine. I learned to distinguish the better wines from the so-so wines and developed my palate. Eventually, I was able to recognize the "breed" in fine wines.

To complement my tasting experiences, I continued to read about wine. According to one story, the great wine writer and winery owner Alexis Lichine participated in a blind tasting of fifteen classified Bordeaux wines. He was able to pick his own wine, Château Prieuré-Lichine, from the group by tasting it. I was shocked. Obviously, he knew that he was drinking Bordeaux wines, but there are hundreds of Bordeaux wines, and to be able to identify precisely which one is yours is not as easy as one might think. Even though I was serious about learning wine, I knew that I had a long way to go.

JoJo continued working for her father, but she spent quite a bit of time learning to cook my Nonna's classic dishes. She would stand next to her with paper and pencil in hand and write down the ingredients and steps so she could make my favorite dishes. She noted how long the pasta cooked, how much olive oil she used, and how long the tomatoes cooked. They tasted Nonna's sauces together, and even compared brands of canned tomatoes. JoJo learned quickly. I thought she was doing it all to please me, but the truth of the matter was that she was looking forward to cooking for our own family.

About a year after JoJo and I were married, my father-in-law recognized the passion I had developed for wine and asked me to join Pacific Wine Company. "I believe you will have more opportunity to grow in the wine business if you come to work for me," he said. "I think this is the place for you, and I would like to have you here." As soon as the words were spoken, I absently wondered if Bob Mondavi had had something to do with Paterno's offer.

Paterno was a formidable man, a very hard worker, and a great competitor. His offer really put me on the spot. By that time, my uncle had returned to Brooklyn, and my father depended on me more than ever. Leading Liquor Marts was growing: We had hired more people and had been considering opening other locations.

I was uneasy about telling my father, "My father-in-law wants me to go to work at Pacific Wine. What do you think?" When I finally broached the subject with him, it certainly wasn't a happy moment. He could find additional help, of course, but it wouldn't be the same.

But his response was typical of the kind of man he was. Without hesitating for a moment, he said, "It's good for you to go. The wine distribution is going to grow."

It took a lot of courage for him to say that. If one of my sons told me that he had a chance to go work for someone else, I doubt I'd accept it as easily as he had. As much as he needed me, as hard as he was working, he simply said, "If going to Pacific Wine is an opportunity for you, you should take it. We'll just hire another person or two. You go there and see how you like it. If it doesn't work out, remember: you can always come back."

There was so much to admire about my father. He was an honest man with character and tenacity. He'd given up everything he'd ever known to establish his business in Chicago. But he did it—he went into a business that he didn't know very much about, and he made it work. He opened the store at nine in the morning, locked it up at ten at night, and was rarely in bed before midnight. He worked like hell and made a lot of sacrifices. He didn't say a lot, but he was really smart about people and didn't take advantage, even when he had the opportunity to do so. In my heart, I knew he had come to Chicago to open the store just to get me involved, give me a business opportunity, and get me out of Florida.

With my father's blessing, I accepted Paterno's offer. Bob Mondavi was the first person to call with congratulations—validating my earlier suspicion that he had suggested the job in the first place.

———————

My father and Anthony Paterno were both very family-oriented men, but they were also quite different. My father-in-law left school after the third grade and worked hard all his life—first, he put in long hours every day on the railroad, and then later, after settling in Chicago, he toiled seven days a week in his grocery store. For him, everything was always a struggle, and his objective was always to win.

Paterno's store was a typical Italian grocery on the corner of Grand and Western Avenues. He kept live chickens in coops along the Western Avenue side. Half the store was a butcher shop, and the other half featured displays of tomatoes, gallon cans of Fieramosca and Filippo Berio olive oil, and prosciutto and cheeses hanging from the ceiling. At some point along the way, he decided to transition the grocery business into a liquor and wine shop.

When JoJo was a baby, her mother kept her in a buggy while she worked in the grocery store most of the day. Lena did the bookkeeping and paid all the bills. She was also a wonderful hostess, and her home was always open to friends and Paterno's business associates alike. The Paterno and Terlato families both had a superb work ethic. Improving their station in life was paramount, and creating opportunities for the family was an obsession. Twelve-hour days weren't a sacrifice; instead, they were loaded with welcome opportunities.

In 1942, Paterno expanded the store, adding one of the first commercial pizza parlors in Chicago. Paterno's pizza was so popular that people would wait for an hour or more to get a table. Still more lined up outside for take-out pizza.

Four years later, Paterno bought out his partner in his other business, the Pacific Wine Company. Pacific Wine was one of thirty-five wine-bottling companies operating in the city of Chicago at that time. The business was located at 836 South Sherman Street, just adjacent to the Rock Island railroad tracks; Pacific's bulk wine was delivered by tank cars that were switched to tracks that ran alongside the back of the building. Pacific employees would pump the wine from the tank cars into Pacific's storage tanks, and then bottle the wines under either a Pacific Wine label or a private label for retailers, such as Armanetti.

My brother-in-law, John, ran Pacific's bottling line, and Pacific also employed a sales manager, Gene Servillo, who also handled the pricing. One of the salesmen and I also pitched in at my father-in-law's pizza parlor on Friday and Saturday nights, and I got firsthand experience making pizzas.

My day job was primarily focused on selling Pacific's wines to liquor stores. My territory included the stores that sold cheap pints of wine on Madison Street, better known at the time as Skid Row. It was a lousy neighborhood, with dirty streets and garbage-filled sidewalks. Drifters and down-and-outers slept in doorways, begging for a cigarette or a pint. Making sales calls in a suit, starched white shirt, cufflinks, and tie, I didn't exactly fit in.

Each of Chicago's thirty-five wine-bottling companies had about ten different labels, which meant that there were about 350 brands of privately labeled wine available for purchase. Pacific bottled its own brands of Burgundy, Chianti, and Chablis, as well as more than twenty other labels. The competition was intense.

There was no incentive for any bottling company to sell better wine because of the market's tremendous price sensitivity. If the price went up as little as ten cents, the buyer would choose a cheaper option. Restaurants wanted nothing more than red and white wine that was drinkable and could sell for about a dollar per six-ounce glass. The restaurants paid about seventy-nine cents for each gallon, and since there are 128 ounces in a gallon, they'd make $12 on a seventy-nine-cent investment.

A few restaurant owners were willing to taste one wine against the other and pay a little bit more for quality. But by and large, restaurateurs had only one question: "What does it cost by the ounce?" If I told them three cents an ounce, they would buy it. If the wine was five cents an ounce, I had less of a chance. Selling the wine that Pacific bottled was a world apart from selling Château Lafite 1955 in my father's store.

After about six months at Pacific Wine, I told my father-in-law, "I would rather go back to my father's store. I don't want to be doing this all my life. If we raise the price of a case of wine by only fifty cents, we lose the business. Nobody cares about quality. All that matters is the price."

"Well, what do you want to do?" he asked.

"I want to do what I know best—selling good wines, the wines I enjoy drinking. That's what I did in my father's store."

"How do you think you're going to do that at Pacific?"

"To start, I want to bring in some really good wines to sell to restaurants. We must offer wines that the better restaurants will be interested in. It'll take us in a different direction."

My father-in-law was unconvinced, but from what I had seen on the menus of better restaurants and read about in gourmet magazines, I was convinced that wine was about to transform from a commodity to a serious product. The wine lists of fine restaurants, like the Buttery at the Ambassador West Hotel, included selections by Alexis Lichine (for example, Château d'Yquem 1949 for $10), but I also believed the wine and liquor business was ready for change. I believed it would soon shift its focus from selling cheap intoxicants to storefronts, taverns, and saloons to distributing wines to restaurants that wanted to offer a premium experience. I also knew that local wine bottling would soon be a thing of the past. Petri, Roma, and Mission Bell had begun to bottle wine where the grapes were grown in California, and Charles Krug was also bottling its own wines under the CK Mondavi label. Soon locally bottled jug wines would become obsolete, as more and more California wineries realized the economic advantages of bottling their own wines and shipping them across the country.

I thought we could begin growing a business with restaurants by building up a few of the quality wines Pacific Wine already offered, such as CK Mondavi. We weren't doing much with it, because California-bottled wines were so much more expensive than the bulk wine that was our bread and butter. (A bottle of locally bottled wine sold for $.99 a gallon, and CK Mondavi sold for $1.98.) Pacific had also acquired the right to sell the Italian imports Mirafiore and Bolla for Chicago, so aggressively marketing them could be the beginning of a move in the right direction.

I told my father-in-law that I would like Pacific to sell French wines as well. I personally enjoyed many French selections, especially the wines of Bouchard Père & Fils Burgundy. I'd first tasted the 1955 Bouchard Le Corton at the Sheraton Blackstone with Guy Armanetti, who had become a great friend of mine. That evening, Guy and I had just won the doubles handball championship at the Illinois Athletic Club, and we celebrated in the dining room of the Blackstone with beef Stroganoff and the Bouchard. It was one of

the most memorable wines I had ever tasted, and I dreamed that
Pacific Wine could become Bouchard's Illinois distributor.

My father-in-law was not very excited about French wines, but
he didn't say no. I immediately called Vintage Wine in New York
City and made an appointment to meet Henry Behar, the U.S.
importer for Bouchard Père & Fils.

It was the spring of 1958. I wanted JoJo, who was having a
rough time after miscarrying our first child, to come to New York
City with me; I thought the trip would do her good and distract
her from the loss we both felt. We stayed at the Sherry Netherland,
one of New York's finest hotels at the time.

In addition to Behar, I also contacted Ercole Sozzi, who
represented Bolla Veronese Wines in the United States. My father-
in-law had acquired the Bolla brand a few years earlier, and Sozzi
knew him and the rest of the Paterno family well. Sozzi was
especially fond of JoJo, and he and I quickly became friends.

Sozzi was a very distinguished Renaissance man, with white
wavy hair and a certain elegance about him. During the 1950s,
he assembled a portfolio of some of the better wines from Italy. At
the time, it was a short list, because many of the best wines were
not available for export. Bolla was his most important brand. But
wine was not his only passion: In the past, he had also brought
Italian sculptors to the United States and helped them exhibit their
work.

When Sozzi heard that we were coming to New York, he invited
JoJo and me to lunch. I doubt I'll ever forget that particular lunch,
in fact, because it was the first time I'd ever eaten frog legs. We
dined at La Forchetta, and gentleman that he was, Sozzi offered to
order. The entrée arrived, and suddenly I was staring at a plate of

cuisses de grenouilles. There was no escape. I couldn't offend Sozzi, so I told myself that if I liked French wines as much as I did, I would also have to acquire a taste for some of the traditional dishes of France. I told myself that I was eating chicken and drank a lot of wine. Needless to say, JoJo enjoyed the whole experience.

It was a long time before I ordered frog legs again, but over the years Sozzi became a model for me. I will always remember his cosmopolitan view of the world, his kindness, and his wisdom—he often advised me to slow down and spend more time reading books about something other than my usual obsession, wine.

JoJo spent the next day shopping, and my appointment with Henry Behar was scheduled for three thirty. I decided to spend the few hours before the meeting at the famous wine shop Sherry's (now Sherry-Lehmann) to check out its inventory. Sherry's had a reputation of having the best selection of imported wines in the country, and I was not disappointed. It was like a library of wine.

I was strolling the aisles, intently scribbling down the names on many of the labels, when a well-dressed gentleman came up to me and said, "I can't help noticing that you're looking at every bottle in the store. What are you looking for, and where are you from?" I told him I was visiting from Chicago and was interested in the wines in the shop.

"Are you in the business?" he asked. I told him that I was a wine distributor who had come to New York to get the Bouchard Père & Fils brand for our distributorship. He examined me more closely and said, "My name's Henry Behar. Bouchard Père & Fils belongs to me."

It was two o'clock, and he suggested that we get something to eat. At that point, I knew our meeting had already started. We ate, drank, talked a lot about wine, and got to know each other. Eventually, Behar made me an offer.

"I'll give you a hundred cases of Bouchard on the condition that you take another wine I've just brought to the United States." He told me about a very interesting Portuguese rosé wine in a crock bottle. I wanted Bouchard no matter what the conditions, so I agreed to take on the rosé and twenty-five cases of a 1937 Setubal Muscatel, also from Portugal.

When I told my father-in-law that I had had gotten Bouchard, he was surprised, but happy for me. When I added that there were a few conditions—"I also got 800 cases of Portuguese rosé in a crock bottle"—he asked, "Are you crazy?"

Armanetti's stores were big retailers of Bouchard, as were Austin Liquors and Foremost Liquors, and they agreed to take on the rosé if we supplied them with Bouchard. Thus, quite by accident, we launched the phenomenon that became Lancers Rosé in Chicago. Before long, it appeared on the wine lists of Le Petit Gourmet, the President's Walk, and the Seven Continents at O'Hare, as well as many other local restaurants. The little crock bottle of Portuguese rosé had hit the market at just the right time, and it became a million-case brand in the United States.

Soon after acquiring Bouchard, I struck a deal with another importer to distribute French wines in Chicago. We also acquired Mateus, another rosé from Portugal, and we became the Blue Nun distributor for Illinois when we purchased another Illinois distributorship, Recher Wine Company. In a period of a few years, we had assembled four of what were to become the largest selling restaurant wines of the late 1950s. Our distribution of Bolla Wines in Italian restaurants was growing, and we were making inroads in French restaurants with the Bouchard as well. We were making significant progress, but we still had a long way to go.

During one of Bob Mondavi's business trips to Chicago, he invited me to dinner at the Porterhouse Room. After dinner, we went for a walk and chatted.

Mondavi said, "Tony, someday, we'll go into a restaurant, and just like in Europe, there will be a bottle of wine on every table."

Mondavi's offhand prediction made an impression on me. Even though our conversation occurred fifty years ago, I remember it like it was yesterday. Of course, he was right.

I was beginning to understand that one day, wine would be as important in America as it was in Europe. We'd already locked up the three most popular restaurant wines in America, so it was time to plan ahead. Lancers, Mateus, and Blue Nun were the bridge wines that would make the United States the largest consumer of fine wines in the world. We'd made an entrance, and now our next step was to put together a portfolio of wines people would aspire to drink during the next twenty years.

As Mondavi and I strolled around the block, I thought that one day, Paterno would be the most important distributor for quality wines in Chicago. I wondered, "Where should we start? France, Italy, Germany, Spain … ?"

I didn't have to wait long for the answer to come.

Paterno's Pan Pizza

This is the Paterno-Terlato family recipe for the original pizza served at the Grand and Western pizzeria when it opened in the late 1930s. Since that time, it has changed slightly in the making, but not in its appeal to pizza aficionados.

Serves 6

Dough:

1 teaspoon sugar

1 envelope active dry yeast

1 cup warm water

1 tablespoon melted butter

1 teaspoon salt

2¼ cups, divided, plus 2 tablespoons flour

1. Dissolve sugar and yeast in water in the bowl of an electric mixer. Let stand until bubbles form. Add butter, salt, and 1 cup of the flour. Mix on low speed with dough-hook attachment until combined. Add remaining flour, about ½ cup at a time, until the dough clings to the hook and gathers from the sides of the bowl.

2. Knead 2 minutes longer or knead by hand on a floured surface until soft and elastic but still slightly sticky. Place in lightly oiled bowl, turn dough to oil top, and cover with plastic wrap. Let rise at room temperature until double in size, about 1½ hours. Punch dough down; cover with plastic wrap. Let rest for 5 minutes.

Topping:

1½ cups canned crushed tomatoes with added puree

12 slices (9 ounces) mozzarella cheese

2 ounces pepperoni, thinly sliced or roasted red peppers, thinly sliced

¼ cup sliced black olives

1½ teaspoon dried oregano

Freshly ground pepper, to taste

¼ cup freshly grated Parmigiano-Reggiano cheese

2 tablespoons olive oil

1. Heat oven to 400°F. Stretch and press dough into greased 17 × 12-inch baking sheet. Prick dough with fork. Spread crushed tomatoes over dough. Top with mozzarella cheese. Add pepperoni and olives. Sprinkle with oregano, pepper, and Parmigiano-Reggiano cheese. Drizzle olive oil over top.

2. Bake on lowest oven rack until browned, about 35 minutes. Turn oven off and slide pizza off pan, setting it directly on oven rack. Leave in oven 5 minutes. Remove to a cutting board and cut into squares.

SUGGESTED WINES

Santa Margherita Chianti Classico, Mischief & Mayhem Bourgogne Pinot Noir, Tangley Oaks Merlot.

FLORENTINE RAVIOLI

In Florence, JoJo and I visited a small family restaurant close to the Academy where we had gone to see Michelangelo's David. We stopped in and saw this on their menu—a ravioli without pasta—and it was terrific. We both speak Italian, of course, so I asked for the recipe. The owner was hesitant, but she gave it to us, and it has been a family favorite for over 40 years.

MAKES APPROXIMATELY 90 1-TABLESPOON BALLS

2 pounds chopped spinach (frozen)

3 pounds hand-dipped ricotta

¾ cup grated Parmigiano-Reggiano cheese

2 eggs

3 cups all-purpose (or Wondra) flour

1. Thaw spinach and then re-chop and thoroughly squeeze out the water.

2. Put ricotta through the finest plate in a food mill. Combine all ingredients, except flour. Using a 1-tablespoon ice cream scoop, scoop balls out of ricotta mixture and roll in flour to coat. Repeat.

3. In a large pot, fill halfway with water and bring to a boil. Reduce hear to a simmer and season with salt. Place the balls in the simmering water and cook until the ravioli floats. Allow ravioli to cook for 1 minute and remove. Serve immediately with a tomato sauce or Bolognese sauce.

SUGGESTED WINES
Ca' del Bosco Pinèro, Il Poggione San Leopoldo, Domaine Terlato & Chapoutier Shiraz-Viognier

Sicily: Land of Contrasts

QUALITY IS NOT AN ACT. IT IS A HABIT.

—Aristotle

BY LATE OCTOBER OF 1958, JOJO WAS PREGNANT again. Fearing another miscarriage, her doctor ordered her to spend the last four months of her pregnancy in bed. We temporarily decamped and moved in with my in-laws in Lincolnwood, where her mother and sister could keep her company and distract her from the boredom of bedrest. In addition, she did a good bit of Pacific Wine's bookkeeping from her bed to keep her mind busy.

It got a bit crowded in that house, so my father-in-law suggested that he and I take a trip to Italy to visit some wineries and journey down the boot of Italy to Sicily, home to the Terlato and Paterno families. It would be my first trip to Europe, and I didn't know what to expect.

In 1953, JoJo had made the transatlantic trip on the *Andrea Doria* with her family to visit her grandparents, who lived near Paterno, a city in the Catania region of Sicily. She had told me about the orange groves that surround the city and the old Norman castle that overlooks the town. I soon discovered that the thriving wine businesses that ranged from the Italian Alps to the island of Sicily grabbed my attention much more than the beautiful scenery.

We landed in Milan and went first to Canelli, a small town in Piedmont. There, the Gancia family had been producing "Spumante," a sparkling wine, since 1865. Vittorio Gancia's grandfather Carlo had worked for Piper-Heidsieck in France in the mid-1800s, and upon his return home, he started the sparkling wine business in Italy. His son Lamberto Valarino Gancia brought it to fame with the creation of Gancia Asti Spumante, and the name Gancia became synonymous with Italian sparkling wine.

The *castello* (castle) Gancia loomed over the town, where almost everybody worked for Gancia, Martini Rossi, or Cinzano—all competing companies at the time. Almost everybody in Canelli was involved in the wine business in some way or other, and the restaurants and motels were rather small. On the other hand, Turin, the largest city in the region, was very aristocratic, with old palaces, cathedrals, and remnants of its former majesty as the capital of the Savoy kingdom. Piedmont was filled with history and beauty, and during that first visit, my head was spinning.

Restaurants were plentiful in Turin, and it was November, the season for white truffles. Today, white truffles are stratospheric in price. In 1958, they were somewhat more accessible, but they were pricier than I thought any mushroom could ever be. One evening, my father-in-law and I went to dinner, and he told me, "We're going to have white truffles tonight." It was a first for me. The waiter came out with plates of fettuccine with a little butter on it, and he finely shaved the white truffle over the pasta with a fine-bladed mandoline that is used only for truffles. The taste and the strong aroma were one-of-a-kind and delicious.

When we finished our dinner, my father-in-law got the bill. He looked at it for a few minutes and then called the waiter over to our table.

He pointed to the pasta charge and said, "What is this?"

The waiter replied, "You kept saying, '*Mettere, mettere*.' Every time I was shaving more, it was costing you money. What do you think, you get all of that white truffle for nothing?"

The experience became a joke between us, because during Italy's white-truffle season, you eat truffles morning, noon, and night. You have many dishes with white truffles because they are only available for such a short time, and you pay dearly for them.

One of my father-in-law's goals for the trip to Piedmont was to find a Barolo to bring back to Chicago. We'd already visited three or four wineries before we met Renato Ratti, the owner of the Abbazia dell'Annunziata in La Morra, the heart of Barolo. Ratti's hospitality was warm, and we enjoyed tasting many of his wines. Ratti, a true Renaissance man, was also a scholar of Italian wine; he owned a vast collection of books about the wines of Italy. I liked him immediately.

Our next stop was a cooperative, where farmers all brought their grapes, blended them, and made wine. My father-in-law, who was, after all, a wine bottler, tasted the wine and said, "I think we'll take the wine from this cooperative. Then we'll have a Barolo to sell that's not too expensive. We'll give them an order." I was shocked. We had just tasted Ratti's wines, and there was clearly no comparison.

I thought carefully before speaking. "I really don't think we should buy the wine from the cooperative. We should take Renato's wines."

"You know Ratti's wine is twice the price?" he said.

"Yes, but it is more than twice as good. I can sell more of Ratti's wine than the co-op's wine."

Unfortunately, Paterno was as stubborn as I was. "No, no, no. We're buying from the cooperative. That's final."

"If we're going to come to Italy together to buy wine and you're going to just tell me what you're going to do, then maybe you shouldn't bring me next time."

I guess I made my point. He paused and then reluctantly said, "Okay, we'll go back to both places tomorrow."

We returned to Ratti's the next day, and my father-in-law told him, "I want to buy wine from the cooperative, and my son-in-law wants to buy wine from you. Can you give me a better price?"

"I can't give you a better price. That's my price. Remember, the production is very small," Ratti replied.

Now my father-in-law was in a pickle. I didn't want the cooperative wine. Ratti would not reduce his price.

Paterno asked me, "What do you want to do?"

We bought Ratti's wine, and my father-in-law didn't resist. In fact, over the years, he and Ratti became good friends. Ratti soon became the head of the Barolo consortium and wrote the definitive book on single-vineyard Barolos.

The next day, Ratti took me to lunch and gave me a little education on the wines of Europe.

"I will show you the zone where all the greatest wines of Europe come from, and why." He opened his briefcase and pulled out a map of Europe. On it, he drew two jagged lines from Portugal to Russia. "All of the area above the top line is too cold to produce wine. Most of the area between these two lines has an elevation of approximately 600 meters [more than 1,900 feet] above sea level. The area includes Burgundy, Bordeaux, Champagne, Mosel, the Rheingau, parts of Switzerland, and the northern parts of Portugal and Spain. Because of the elevation and other conditions, the days are warm and the evenings are cool. The cooler evening temperatures result in wines that are fruity and fresh and have good acidity. These wines differ in quality from vintage to vintage, and the wines' varietals can be identified by a reasonably knowledgeable wine drinker."

Ratti continued, "The region below the bottom line has a Mediterranean climate, with more than 100 days each year when the temperature exceeds 37 degrees [Celsius, approximately 100 degrees Fahrenheit]. After five years in the bottle, all of the wines produced in this zone, which includes the entire southern part of Europe, are indistinguishable. In fact, it is almost impossible to identify the grape varietal."

I was fascinated. Ratti paused, then added, "Wines grown in regions that fall between these two lines are like fresh fruit, and because of the heat, those grown below the bottom line are similar to dried fruit. In the Mediterranean zone, of course, there are a few exceptions, because some vineyards lie above 600 meters, and thus the climate is cool enough to grow a wine like those from Northern Europe."

That trip to Italy was a revelation. I wanted to import the best wines of Piedmont, and I wasn't interested in buying the lowest-priced wine in a particular category. But I was beginning to learn that price versus quality was going to be an ongoing issue between Paterno and me.

I now realize that my father-in-law's reason for taking me to Italy was not only to get my opinion about the wines he was buying but also to educate me about our shared heritage: to see where my parents had been born, visit the towns where my grandparents had lived, and meet people who knew them. Paterno also showed me where he was born, where he had lived, where he had gone to school, and above all, where the cemetery was. (For some reason, Italian relatives always take the younger generations to the cemeteries to show them their relatives' final resting places. So I saw many of my relatives, one way or the other.)

In Sicily, we visited a little town called Vizzini and stayed at Paterno's sister's home. The house was large, but it was very cold and had no heat. I will never forget it: the very moment the sun went down, it became freezing cold. As we sat in the dining room for dinner the first evening, my teeth began to chatter.

The nights were another kind of horror story. Most Sicilian families had a primitive heating device called a *scaldaletto*, a big, round, copper pan with hot coals in it. They would put slates of bamboo over the top of the *scaldaletto* and put it under the covers of the bed to warm it up. It did its job, and the bed was nice and warm when I got into it. By three in the morning, however, I was freezing.

I also remember taking a shower in the cold bathroom. (The only way to get hot water was to turn the stove on and heat it in a large pot.) I couldn't get dry fast enough.

My father-in-law loved every minute of our visit. He had a great sense of humor, told jokes easily, and peppered his conversations with folk sayings in Italian as well as English. One of his favorites was, "Don't spit up into the sky, because it will come back in your eye." Paterno was also an expert card player, and he spent every afternoon in Vizzini's *piazza* (plaza) playing an Italian version of poker with the townsmen. Paterno was tremendously respected in the town. He had been very generous and supportive and was considered a patron of the town. He had paid for the renovation of the church's façade, financed some of the public buildings, and supported two of the orphanages.

So what did I think of Italy after that first trip with my father-in-law? It was important for me to see where my family had lived and worked before immigrating to the States. Seeing my father-in-law's continuing support of his relatives in Sicily firsthand gave me a greater sense of family just before I became a father myself.

Our son William was born in February 1959, and our second son, John, came along thirteen months later. They were the first generation of the Terlato–Paterno patrimony.

Fettuccine with Shaved White Truffles

In Piedmont, the pasta is rich with egg yolks, wild mushrooms are plentiful in the hills, and during the white truffle season, truffles are shaved over this simple dish as a special enhancement.

Serves 4–5

1 pound dry egg fettuccine

2 tablespoons butter

Salt, to taste

White truffle

1. In a large pot bring water to a boil, add fettuccine, and cook until tender. Strain and pour into a serving dish, mix in some butter and salt.

2. Shave truffles over the top and serve.

Suggested Wines

Rochioli Chardonnay, Bollinger Champagne Special Cuvée

SAFFRON BOW TIES

Although Italian saffron, zafferano, *is usually sold in powdered form, packaged in little envelopes, more readily available saffron threads are an easy substitute in this simple pasta dish. Of course, truffle oil makes it special, as does a cool glass of white wine.*

SERVES 6

1 pound bow tie pasta

2 tablespoons salted butter

3 ounces heavy cream or half-and-half, at room temperature

1½ teaspoons saffron threads, dissolved in 1½ tablespoons veal stock

½ cup grated fresh Parmigiano-Reggiano cheese

1½ teaspoons truffle oil

1½ tablespoons salt

Freshly ground black pepper

1. In a large pot, bring 3 quarts of salted (1½ tablespoons) water to a rolling boil. As the water is heating, place a large serving bowl over the pot to warm the bowl. Once the water is boiling, add the bow tie pasta and stir occasionally, cooking until firm. (Bow tie pasta noodles need approximately 10 minutes to cook.) Drain pasta and place in the warmed serving bowl.

2. Add butter, cream, saffron, veal stock, and truffle oil to the pasta. Toss and cover for 1 minute to let rest.

3. Transfer pasta to warm pasta dishes. Sprinkle lightly with Parmigiano-Reggiano cheese and freshly ground pepper.

SUGGESTED WINES
Chimney Rock Elevage Blanc, Josmeyer Pinot Gris Hengst

Personally Selected By

TRULY GREAT BURGUNDIES COMBINE A RICH BOUQUET WITH AN AMAZING
VELVETY BIGNESS OF BODY AND ARE BEST APPRECIATED WITH RED
MEAT AND GAME. WE ARE PROUD TO OFFER THIS EXCEPTIONAL LIST OF
ESTATE BOTTLINGS, WINES BOTTLED BY THE GROWER, WHICH HAVE ALL
BEEN SELECTED BY ALEXIS LICHINE, AUTHOR OF *WINES OF FRANCE*.
   —*Wine list at the Pump Room, Ambassador East Hotel Chicago, 1958*

WE PRESENT AMERICA'S FINEST TABLE WINES, PERSONALLY SELECTED BY
FRANK SCHOONMAKER AND BOTTLED AT THE WINERY, UNDER HIS
SUPERVISION. AMONG THEM YOU ARE BOUND TO FIND A FITTING AND
DELICIOUS ACCOMPANIMENT TO THE DISH YOU ORDER.
   —*Wine list at the the Sirloin Room at Stock Yard Inn, 1960*

IN THE LATE 1950S, MANY LANDMARK RESTAURANTS
opened in the United States. In New York City, Pavillon,
Forum of the Twelve Caesars (whose waiters were given a
course on wine by James Beard himself), and La Côte Basque
debuted, and in Chicago, the Pump Room, Jacques, Imperial
House, Italian Village, and Maison Lafite were the finest dining
establishments in town.

Chicago was (as it is today) a city of strong ethnic neighborhoods.
Chicago's Italians, Germans, Greeks, Asians, Scandinavians, Jews,
and Mexicans began to open popular restaurants as well. Pizzeria
Uno was started by two ex-GIs who had fallen in love with pizza
while in Italy during World War II. Berghoff's, a German eatery
in the Loop, had been doing fantastic business since its debut in

1898. Kungsholm, a Swedish restaurant on Rush Street, boasted a downstairs puppet opera theater. Manny's Deli, a 1940s cafeteria and gathering spot, offered delicious corned beef and other ethnic delights. Beer was served in some of these establishments, and others offered long lists of cocktails, but in all but the higher-end restaurants, the drink of choice for almost every meal was coffee. I knew that if I wanted to sell wine to restaurateurs, I had a lot of work to do, but I was convinced that the future of our wine distributing business would begin in restaurants. Industry giants like New York's Taylor Cellars and California's Petri, Italian Swiss Colony, and Roma Wine were focused on making low-cost fortified wine that had no place on restaurant tables.

There were some signs that wine would soon take its rightful place at American dinner tables. As I'd learned working in my father's store, many veterans had learned about wine while serving in Italy, France, and Germany. Many returned to the United States with a taste for wine, and it was gradually becoming associated with fine dining.

As air travel became more commonplace, many Americans traveled to other parts of the globe and became more educated about other cuisines and wines. However, some negative attitudes that had prevailed since Prohibition still lingered, and cultural divides remained between sweet and dry wines, high-alcohol and low-alcohol wines, and bulk and premium wines. Many believed the only good wines were imported from Europe and were reserved for the knowledgeable few.

Leading the way in the emerging fine-wine industry, two champions of European wines beat the drums on both sides of the Atlantic: Frank Schoonmaker and Alexis Lichine. Serving as buyers, sellers, exporters, importers, and even winemakers themselves, Schoonmaker and Lichine had helped America's leading restaurants stock their cellars. (Schoonmaker even designed wine glasses to be sold alongside his wines in Bloomingdales' stores.)

Both men had worked together for a time in 1938, when Lichine had been the executive vice president of sales for Frank Schoonmaker's wine importing firm. Schoonmaker and Lichine both served the United States in intelligence roles during World War II, and after 1946, they went their separate ways and competed with one another.

By the mid-1950s, Schoonmaker and Lichine were the two most important suppliers of quality European wine to the United States. Lichine had offices in Margaux and Long Island City and offered one of the finest collections of French Burgundies and Bordeaux coming into the United States. Schoonmaker specialized in German wines, but he had a handsome selection of Burgundies and Bordeaux as well.

In 1960, I had the good luck to meet Lichine at a black-tie dinner in New York City. I don't remember what the occasion was, but traffic delays made me forty-five minutes late for the dinner. A hostess greeted me at the door, saying, "We thought you weren't coming, so we gave away your seat. Let's see if I can find you another." After what seemed like ages, she returned and said, "I found a seat for you."

I followed her to a table where everyone was a stranger to me, except one. I immediately recognized Lichine, a distinguished, good-looking, and tall gentleman with brown hair and a long, thin face. The seat next to him was empty—I couldn't believe my luck. Gentleman that he was, he extended his hand and introduced himself. I told him, "I know who you are."

I was about twenty years younger than he was, but as strange as it seems to me now, we started to talk like old friends. I felt completely at ease in his company and soon forgot that he was a cosmopolitan celebrity—Moscow born and Paris raised—who had seen more of life than I certainly had. We talked for hours about wine, his three-year-old firm, Alexis Lichine & Company, and the half-million bottles of wine he shipped to the United States each year bearing the label "Selected by Alexis Lichine."

Lichine clearly understood that I was a Francophile, and he told me about many of the different French wines he was exporting to the States. We discussed the huge opportunities for high-quality French wines in Chicago, and that I was trying to broaden Pacific Wine's French portfolio. For good measure, I also let him know that I always drank wines selected by him whenever I had dinner at the Pump Room or the Sherman House's Well of the Sea.

After dinner, Lichine invited me to join him at a party at the Russian Tea Room. The restaurant was very fashionable, and everyone recognized Lichine. I felt like a nobody, but I didn't care. We ate caviar, tasted quite a bit of wine, and, of course, talked about wine until two in the morning. As we left the Russian Tea Room, Lichine turned to me and said, "Tony, you're going to be my distributor in Chicago." I could barely contain my delight.

Lichine dealt directly with the French wineries. He would visit each château personally, telling the owner, "I'd like to represent your brand worldwide." If the owner and Lichine reached an agreement, the brand would become part of Alexis Lichine & Company. In those days, it was hard to find an agency in the United States that was willing to take on all of his wines, so he would sell them directly to distributors in each state. The distributors sold to retailers and restaurants, who in turn sold to consumers. Lichine's three-tiered system was very effective, and his brand quickly became well known and well respected.

After my evening with Lichine in New York, I corresponded with him often by mail. After four or five months had passed since our last correspondence, Lichine's sales manager for the United States, Basil Winston, called me. He told me, "I can't meet you in Chicago because we already have a distributor there. You'll have to meet me in Detroit."

We made the arrangements, and I flew to Detroit a few days later. It was like a Mike Hammer movie. Winston sat in a corner booth at a restaurant on a pier.

"Basil Winston?"

He replied, "Anthony Terlato?" It didn't take him long to get to the point. "Alexis wants you to be our distributor in Chicago. Let's talk about what you plan to order."

I interpreted Winston's comment as a challenge. I laughed and replied, "You write the opening order. That way, there won't be any argument about how many cases I have to buy."

Winston looked shocked. Our discussion was completed in less than five minutes. We had a leisurely dinner, and afterward he wrote up the order—a big one. I didn't care. I knew we could sell Lichine's selections. He had just published *The Wines of France*, which would become the wine bible of the 1960s. I knew I had a slam-dunk.

Lichine had just begun to use the *pot* (pronounced "poh") bottle for his Chardonnay, Cabernet Sauvignon, and Rosé d'Anjou. The bottles were clear glass, attractively shaped, and showed off the color of the wines. Each of the wines retailed for $1.98 a bottle.

Chicagoans fell in love with the *pot* bottle. We devised an incentive program for Chicago restaurateurs that offered three free cases with every ten-case order. Sales were so hot that soon, retailers were getting thirty-five free cases for every hundred-case order, and stores all over the city were putting up large floor displays of Lichine wines. In a few years, we were the largest Lichine distributor in the country. Our success inspired Frank Schoonmaker to join Lichine at Pacific Wine Company, so we suddenly had two of the most influential wine importers of the time in our portfolio.

The Lichine and Schoonmaker wines were considered superior to almost all others, to be sure, but they were also considered high-end, and thus expensive. As a result, some restaurants were reluctant to offer them. I had to prove to them that it was a worthwhile risk, because the profit margins on the quality wines were better.

Eventually, I had the more reluctant restaurateurs simply taste the wine alongside some of the other wines they were selling. I'd tell them, "Let's do it blind. We'll cover up the bottles so you can't tell which is which. If you like mine better, will you put it on your list?" Some said maybe, and others said yes. At that point, I'd lay my pencil and paper on the bar—a symbol that I would prevail, and that I would write that order.

Maybe I was a good salesman, or maybe the product sold itself, but my strategy got their attention—and most importantly, it got them to taste the wine. I didn't want to talk about price. I wanted them to choose the better wine *because* it was better.

A few years earlier, we had made great progress in Chicago's Italian restaurants with Bolla; now we were capturing the French restaurants and fine hotels like the Sherman House, the Drake, and the Edgewater Beach with the wines of Lichine and Schoonmaker. We quickly built a high-quality portfolio of Bordeaux and Burgundy wines and even landed Roederer's Cristal Champagne, which was new to Chicago. We gave unparalleled service to our customers, including waitstaff training, next-day delivery, and knowledgeable salespeople who never watched the clock. Twelve-hour days were the norm. I worked the high-end restaurants— places like Armando's, Agostino's, the Imperial House, Riccardo's,

Italian Village, the Gold Star Inn, Jacques, Maison Lafite, and Gianotti's.

Our new direction was a world apart from our existing business. None of the other thirty-five bottlers of California wines in the city was pushing high-end labels like Roederer Champagne, French Burgundies and Bordeaux, or Soave Bolla to sell in restaurants for $12 a bottle. (At the time, diners could get a carafe of wine for $1.25 in many restaurants.) I knew it was going to be a tough sell to some restaurants, but I was convinced the future was in quality imported wines. (In the years to come, I found that the future included fine wines from California as well.) Let the local wine bottlers fight it out amongst one another, I thought. I was figuring out how to escape the bottling business altogether, and take Pacific Wine to a whole new level.

Tournedos Rossini

*I don't remember exactly what entrée was served the evening I dined with
Alexis Lichine, but Tournedos Rossini was standard fare in many New
York dining establishments in the 1950s. And the fact that one of Lichine's
"selections" was a 1955 Chambertin seemed to make both an unbeatable
combination. These days, I serve the dish with a bottle of Domaine Terlato &
Chapoutier Malakoff Shiraz or Angelo Gaja Barbaresco.*

SERVES 6

Tournedos:

6 4-ounce beef fillets

1 tablespoon butter

1 tablespoon coarsely ground fresh black peppercorns

Salt, to taste

6 round sourdough croustades toasted in butter

6 slices goose liver pâté

2 black truffles, thinly sliced

1 cup Madeira Sauce

1. On a hot greased grill or cast-iron frying pan, cook fillets to
   desired degree of doneness. Season and set aside on a heated
   plate.

2. Fry croustades in butter, place on six individual serving plates,
   top each with a slice of pâté, place a fillet on each, and garnish
   with truffle slices.

3. Serve with Madeira Sauce on the side.

Madeira Sauce:

2 tablespoons butter

2 tablespoons finely minced shallots

1 cup veal demi-glace

2 tablespoons lemon juice

¼ cup Madeira wine

1. Melt the butter in a saucepan, and sauté the shallots until wilted.

2. Add the demi-glace and lemon juice and bring to a boil and reduce heat. Add the wine and simmer for about five minutes. Serve warm.

Suggested Wines

Domaine Terlato & Chapoutier Malakoff Shiraz, Gaja Barbaresco, Two Hands Aphrodite

The Right Time

IF YOU ALWAYS DO WHAT YOU HAVE ALWAYS DONE, YOU WILL ALWAYS END UP
WHERE YOU HAVE ALWAYS BEEN.

—*Anonymous*

IN RETROSPECT, I CAN CLEARLY SEE THE TURNING point. When President John F. Kennedy took office in 1961, Americans began to see fashion, food, and wine with new eyes. A gift of a silk scarf from Chanel went a long way to please my wife, JoJo. Many folks began to look at wine as something much more than alcohol, and suddenly food was much more important than just nourishment. Rising chef Julia Child's book, *Mastering the Art of French Cooking*, and her TV show, *The French Chef*, drove hordes of women into their kitchens to make traditional French dishes like *coq au vin* and *boeuf Bourguignon*—dishes that seemed incomplete without a bottle of French wine.

It's amazing to me now that it took me so long to get there, but in 1962, I visited France for the first time. By that point, I had become very familiar with the names and wines of the classified growths in Bordeaux, so I was specifically interested in visiting the châteaux Lafite Rothschild, Haut-Brion, Cheval Blanc, and Mouton Rothschild. At the annual dinner of the wine group the Sons of Bacchus on April 26, 1962, at Jacques Restaurant in Chicago, I saw Lichine and told him about my plans to visit

France. He immediately invited me to stay as his guest at one of his vineyards, Château Lascombes, and told me he would have his staff arrange appointments for me to visit the blockbuster châteaux of the Médoc. The time had come for me to go to Bordeaux, and I was ready.

Lichine, along with a list of backers and stockholders, was the principal owner of Château Lascombes in Margaux and Château Prieuré-Lichine in Cantenac. Lichine had spent most of the 1950s restoring the property in Cantenac, making a grand dining room where the old kitchen had once been, and installing modern electricity and plumbing.

Lichine's headquarters were located ten minutes away from Château Prieuré-Lichine in a hundred-year-old two-story stone building on Margaux's Rue du General de Gaulle. Like the château, he had modernized the company's cellars and the building, installing fluorescent lights and electric typewriters. He had begun the enterprise with only three employees, but over time, his staff had grown to thirty, with half working in the offices and the other half in the cellar and shipping rooms. During my stay, Lichine's secretary, Katherine La Louvière, personally drove me to Cos d'Estournel, Beychevelle, Margaux, and many other châteaux. We tasted countless wines in cold cellars and rode around in the hot sunshine from early morning until late in the evening each day.

Most of the châteaux had a routine list of wines available for tasting. Since Lichine had arranged my visits, the châteaux were much more accommodating than usual. I was astonished when some owners opened extremely rare and costly wines from 1945 and 1947 for me to taste. Not to be outdone, Michel Becot, a proprietor in St. Emilion, opened a magnificent bottle of 1929 Château Beausejour. I couldn't quite process it all, but I knew I was experiencing the best wines in the world.

Lichine happened to be in Bordeaux during my visit, and he invited me to lunch the last day of my trip. We met at his office, and before leaving for the restaurant we enjoyed a few glasses of wine together—wonderful vintages of Château Lascombes 1955 and 1959 and some barrel samples of the 1961. During lunch, I mentioned that I admired Lichine's "coffee table," a huge bellows made from staves of wood-aging barrels from Château Lascombes.

A year later, a huge box from France with my name on it arrived at Pacific Wine's loading dock. Elio Guzzardi, our head of shipping and receiving, couldn't imagine what was in it. Inside, I discovered the massive bellows that I had seen in Lichine's office. The attached note read, "I had two of these made, and I want you to have one." I still have the bellows to this day, and it remains a constant reminder of my friendship with Lichine.

My enthusiasm for French wines grew, but I also discovered that French food in the tradition of Escoffier was not for me—there were too many rich sauces and off-putting ingredients for my taste. My upbringing in an Italian household drew me to simpler dishes—the pastas, risottos, grilled meats, and fresh salads of the Italian table. In fact, I never truly embraced French cuisine until the nouvelle cuisine trend was ushered in by Paul Bocuse—its lighter sauces and fresh ingredients cooked to order and presented on individual plates were much more my style. Bocuse's natural approach to move away from heavy cream-based sauces was far more wine friendly as well. I had the pleasure of meeting Bocuse myself through the legendary Chicago chef and owner of Les Nomades, Jovan Trboyevic, who introduced us at a private luncheon at his Le Perroquet restaurant.

During that first trip to Bordeaux, I purchased a lot of wine for Pacific. Coincidentally, around the same time, Robert Mondavi also visited a number of the same Bordeaux châteaux to see firsthand how some French winemakers used new oak barrels for aging and others reused barrels for a few vintages to prevent the flavor of the new oak from affecting the wines. While I was on a buying spree to import hundreds of cases of Bordeaux wines for Pacific, Mondavi was absorbing concepts about fermentation, de-stemming, centrifugal filtration, and the benefits of aging in new French oak barrels versus barrels that had been used for previous vintages.

Under the label Paterno Imports, my father-in-law had begun importing olive oil and using a portion of our wine-bottling equipment to bottle Regina vinegar. I feared it was a very risky venture, with the vinegar being far too close to the wine-bottling operation. Storage space had also become an issue, and my enthusiasm for importing French wines was in direct conflict with his priorities. All that French wine was taking up a lot of our storage area.

The second-guessing began to occur more frequently. At one point, we had four hundred cases of Château Lafite 1959 stored away for future sales. I had paid less than $30 a case, and three years later, it was still sitting in the warehouse, waiting for the right time to sell. Even after only three years, the wine was worth considerably more because of its prized vintage. Paterno came across it during an inventory count and told me, "You've got all that Château Lafite out there. It's taking up space and tying up money. It will take forever to sell it."

I responded, "I could sell it by the end of the day, if I wanted to."

Of course, he retorted, "Let me see you do it."

Before we went home that evening, I sold 300 of the cases. (I held onto the last hundred because I knew I could get a lot more for it later.) As I was leaving the office that night, I stuck my head in my father-in-law's office.

"By the way, 300 cases of the Lafite will ship tomorrow. I sold it for $150 a case. I kept 100 because in the next year or so, I'll be able to sell it for $300 a case."

Paterno's interest was in selling volume, and mine was in selling quality. We argued and made up many times over; I threatened to leave often, and one time, I actually did—for two months. I started my own company, Vintage Wine. Mondavi joined me in the venture, introducing his new wines—Bob's Red and Bob's White. Along with him came a number of other suppliers and a few of Pacific's best employees.

One day, I got a call from an accountant who worked for the firm that did Pacific Wine's bookkeeping. We arranged a meeting, and during our conversation, he casually mentioned that I shouldn't stay in Chicago and compete against the family business, and that perhaps I should consider moving to another state. He also intimated that the suggestion had come from my father-in-law. JoJo, who was in the office helping out with the bookkeeping and files, overheard the conversation.

She left before I did, and we never discussed the incident. Years later, I learned that JoJo had left my office and gone straight to her father.

She demanded, "Who's so afraid Tony will succeed that they want us to leave town? Not you, I hope."

Paterno asked what she was talking about, so she repeated the conversation that had taken place earlier that day. He told her that he knew nothing about it, and he added confidentally that he had personally guaranteed my loan at the bank.

Paterno strolled into my office the next morning. We exchanged greetings, and he said, gruffly, "I want you to close up this place and come back where you belong." I was shocked, but glad. Sometimes you have to give up the past and look to the future.

Although we didn't always see eye-to-eye, I respected my father-in-law immensely. He came to the United States at sixteen with only a few dollars in his pocket and succeeded on pure commitment, hard work, determination, and desire. After his only son, John, died of cancer in 1961, I knew he was counting on me to carry on his work. We played golf together every Sunday, often ate lunch together, and JoJo and I brought the kids to my in-laws' home for dinner at least twice a week.

We always knew it would be a contest of wills between the two of us, and that he would always challenge me. For my part, I had proved to him that I was up for any challenge, so in spite of our differences, he made me president of Pacific Wine Company in 1963. I was twenty-nine years old. I firmly believe his decision was his way of showing me that he approved of what I was doing at Pacific Wine.

———————————

By the late 1960s, our sales force had increased significantly, and we'd incorporated under the name Paterno Imports. We were now licensed to import wines and spirits to sell across the country. Shortly after, I was asked to import an almond cream Marsala dessert wine made by a Sicilian wine producer for Chicago distribution. The wine looked and tasted more like a liqueur than a wine. I was intrigued, but I laid down some requirements: We would come up with our own name for the product, we would own that name, and we would distribute it nationwide—not just in Chicago. That was the beginning of Sicilian Gold, the dessert wine that was the forerunner to Amaretto.

Building on its liqueur-like look and taste, we designed a wonderful tall triangular bottle and an attractive label. It took a lot of effort, but we acquired a genuine Sicilian donkey cart to launch Sicilian Gold in various Italian restaurants. The colorful displays attracted a lot of attention.

After we'd sold a fair number of cases of Sicilian Gold, I decided to take the product to the radio waves. I pitched it on the Wally Phillips morning show on WGN Radio in Chicago. Phillips was the king of radio at the time, and everyone listened to his show while driving to work or doing the breakfast dishes. Sales of Sicilian Gold exploded in Chicago.

That year, my father-in-law and I attended the yearly meeting of the Wine Spirits Wholesalers of America in Las Vegas. We didn't know many people there, but my father-in-law knew some of the wine bottlers from around the country. We brought along some cases of our biggest seller, Mirafiore Asti Spumante, and some Sicilian Gold as well. I stayed in our hotel room with the chilled wines, and my father-in-law would grab likely prospects downstairs and bring them up for tastings. While one fellow sipped the wines, my father-in-law went downstairs to bring up another potential customer. He wouldn't let any of them get away, telling them they had to come upstairs and taste what we had. One by one, each tasted Sicilian Gold and said, "This is fantastic. I want it." First, a distributor in New Orleans hopped on the bandwagon, and then a distributor in Houston, John Siragusa, joined him, each buying a 600-case container. The response was always the same: "This is wonderful. What does it sell for?" (At the time, Sicilian Gold was only $2.49 a bottle.) Once again, the simple strategy of having customers taste our wines was working.

We left the convention with important distributors in New Orleans and Houston and moved 1,200 cases of wine, just like that. From there, I took Sicilian Gold to New York, convincing John Magliocco of Peerless Distributing to sell it to the Italian restaurants of New York. Sicilian Gold started to fly. Next, I paid calls to distributors Hubert Opici in New Jersey and, at Bob Mondavi's suggestion, John Leone in Detroit. Eventually, we increased sales to 35,000 cases nationally, which was very big at the time for an imported dessert wine.

We received a substantial offer from another distributor for the brand, but because I believed Sicilian Gold was our ticket to entering the national playing field, we declined. Vittorio Gancia noted the national success of Sicilian Gold and offered us the U.S. agency for his popular Gancia Asti Spumante. Suddenly Paterno Imports was on its way to becoming a serious national agent.

———————

Soon, Pacific Wine and Paterno Imports outgrew the original Pacific bottling facility at 836 South Sherman. We needed more office space for our staff and more storage space for our imported and local wines. In 1966, Paterno contracted to build a 125,000 square-foot state-of-the-art distribution center at 2701 South Western Avenue. I have a vivid memory of my two young sons, Billy and Johnny, sitting on the cornerstone just as construction began.

In 1968, Pacific Wine Company was offered the Chicago distributorship for Italian Swiss Colony wines. It was the number one wine brand in Chicago, with 700,000 cases in sales. As part of the deal the company required us to hire its twenty-seven-man sales force. We agreed, but in retrospect, taking on Swiss Colony was a minor disaster.

While dining out one evening, I recognized four kids in the restaurant's band—they were our Italian Swiss Colony salesmen. A few weeks later, my wife spotted another of our newly acquired salesmen selling shoes at Joseph's Shoe Salon. Yet another salesman was teaching swimming at the local YMCA. I started to check what time the salesmen called in orders. Most of their orders were called in after three o'clock in the afternoon. We had inherited a bunch of moonlighters.

Despite its popularity, we weren't making any money on Italian Swiss Colony wine, and it was hurting our company. A huge company like Walgreens would submit an order for two bottles of Italian Swiss Colony Sherry and two bottles of white Port to fill in a store's inventory. The cost of that type of delivery was excessive. Piecemeal orders were unprofitable, and it made us crazy. Eventually, we came to realize that selling hundreds of thousands of cases of inexpensive wine was a very costly business.

After carefully analyzing the situation, I approached my father-in-law about it. "This brand is killing us," I told him. "Our imported wine business isn't growing anymore because we're too focused on moving an extremely price-sensitive wine. We have to get rid of it, because it will ruin our company."

"You want to give up that many cases of wine a year?"

"I know," I replied.

The next time the representative from Italian Swiss Colony came in, I lowered the boom. "We really don't want to handle Swiss Colony anymore."

He laughed and said, "Come on."

"We don't…"

He cut me off midsentence and asked, "Is your father-in-law here?"

"Yes. He's in his office."

He walked into Paterno's office and said, "Your son-in-law tells me he doesn't want to handle Italian Swiss Colony anymore."

"Yes. That's what my son-in-law wants."

It was a good move. Gallo soon entered the market and crushed Swiss Colony, and the brand no longer exists. It was a reaffirmation that anything *that* price sensitive is destined to fail at the hands of a more efficient or hungrier competitor. In the end, there's no brand loyalty for that type of product, and brand loyalty is where the real staying power comes from.

The Italian Swiss Colony experiment wasn't a total loss. We retained only one of the twenty-seven Italian Swiss Colony salesmen, John Kournetas. Kournetas was a hard worker and understood what I was trying to accomplish. Kournetas became a supervisor, then sales manager, and eventually vice president of Pacific Wine. Today, more than forty years later, we are still together.

Which brings me to an important point: I consider myself very fortunate to have always been surrounded with talented people, and I've had the pleasure of presenting numerous gold watches to employees in return for twenty-five years of dedicated service. Some say I am difficult to work for or too demanding, but I have found that I seem difficult only to people who don't understand their role. I expect people who work for me to go above and beyond in sales, marketing, service, and all other aspects of their work. If employees find me difficult, it's probably because they don't have that particular something that makes them stand out from the crowd, and they shouldn't be working for me.

Once, a human resources manager told me she was having trouble attracting potential employees. She said, "The company is just too demanding."

I replied, "That's great news. That means the candidates you're interviewing don't belong here. We are a good company, but we want to be a great company. Mediocrity has no place here."

———————————

In 1966, Robert Mondavi left his family's Charles Krug Winery because of family issues and built his own Mission-style winery in Napa. Mondavi immediately began to set a new trend of innovation and excellence in California wines. We felt it was important for our business and friendship with him to help his new effort, as the Robert Mondavi brand was one of our first super-premium quality California wines. In 1969, we launched the Robert Mondavi brand in Illinois. I admired Mondavi's salesmanship and strategies for selling wine—especially the way he concentrated on the restaurant trade.

Distributing quality wines had always meant that we had to do a lot of talking to sell them. With Mondavi, we took a different approach that again put the focus on simple tastings. We'd bring along three or four competing wines, such as Italian Swiss Colony or Paul Masson, to each restaurant call, have the bartender set up two glasses of each wine, and say, "Let's taste the difference." There was always a big difference. Mondavi's wines were always more expensive, but people could taste the difference right away.

When it came to sales, we could talk all we wanted, but tasting the wines made all the difference in the world. We were doing blind tastings of wines when no other salesmen were calling on their accounts with bottles of wine in hand. Most would have nothing more than a price sheet and a picture. Our team could say, "I brought two bottles of wine for you." We would always engage them to taste without letting them know which bottle was which until after they'd sampled both.

I decided to take my own sales pitch up a notch. In the late 1950s and early 1960s, most restaurants had a standard beer and cocktail list with perhaps a carafe or half-carafe of red, white, or rosé wine on their food menus, which were reprinted perhaps twice a year. If a Paterno Imports wine wasn't on the menu, it wouldn't be on it for a while, because the restaurant wouldn't reprint the menus just to add or take off one wine.

It occurred to me that I could offer to print new wine lists for the restaurants at no charge. To test the idea, I told a few restaurateurs, "You don't have to have the wine on the food menu anymore. I'll print you a separate wine list, and if you want me to change it every two months, I'll reprint it every two months." It was an inexpensive hook, but no one else was doing exactly the same thing.

During that time, most wine companies offered to print a wine list for a restaurant, but there were hitches—every wine on the list would have to be from that particular company, and the salesmen would have to get authorization for the expenditure from headquarters. I told restaurateurs, "I'll make your wine list, and I'll deliver it to you the next day."

One retorted, "It takes at least a month to get a wine list. You can't print me a list overnight."

I was nonplussed. "You give me the order. I'll have the wine list in your hands the next day when the restaurant opens, and the wine will be delivered that afternoon. If I don't deliver the printed wine list, you don't have to pay for the wine. All I'm asking you to do is just list one wine from my company." I just wanted to get the camel's head into the tent.

"Impossible," the restaurateur replied. I told him I'd be back.

The next day, I bought a small used printing press and taught one of our order takers how to use it. Next, I wrote up descriptions for most of our wines, so it would be easy to insert each restaurant's prices in the standard wine list.

As promised, I returned to the restaurant the following week and told the proprietor, "Are you ready to give me an order for a wine list?"

The strategy worked, and he agreed to include quite a few of our wines on the list—thinking all the while that he'd get them for free. The next morning, the list was in his hands, and the wine was delivered that afternoon. I got priceless free publicity, because the restaurateur told almost everyone in the industry what I had done for him. I quickly found an audience of restaurateurs who were pleased to be able to change the wine list often at no cost to them.

Within a year, we were giving salesmen bonuses if they managed to convince a restaurant to offer wines distributed by Pacific exclusively on their list. Later, we ended up buying a larger printing press to meet the demand for all the wine lists we were receiving. In time, we made the lists larger, adding some information about the wines and an image of the wine's label above some of the selections. Our strategy eventually evolved to include leather-bound wine list covers with the restaurant's name embossed in gold. Any time a restaurateur wanted to change his wine list, we'd simply reprint a page with the change.

While I focused my efforts on Pacific Wine and the restaurant trade, my father-in-law purchased vineyards and a bottling facility in Greve-in-Chianti, near Florence, from Vittorio Gancia. The brand was Mirafiore Chianti Classico, Gancia's second label.

In the nineteenth century, Victor Emmanuel, the first king of a unified Italy, kept a mistress, Rosina, in the house that we'd bought in Greve. In order to give her and their illegitimate son a position in society, he made Rosina the Countess of Mirafiore, and their son became the Count of Mirafiore. As an adult, the count married a young lady whose father was the owner of a noted winery, and he learned the wine trade well. The brand name Mirafiore was created by Victor Emmanuel's son, and it was well-known in Italy when Gancia bought it.

My father-in-law's goal was to bottle competitively priced wines under the Mirafiore label in 750-ml and 1.5-liter bottles. Reluctantly, I joined the effort. While Paterno continued to produce familiar Chianti in straw baskets, I formulated a wine called Mirafiore Reserve a Del Conte, which sold for $4.98 a fifth—really quite expensive at the time, but the wine was superb. In this way, we both accomplished our goals.

It was an interesting venture, but running a winery in Italy as an absentee owner had its challenges. As he grew older, Paterno began to stay at the winery for three months a year. JoJo and our boys, who were in grammar school at the time, joined the Paternos there for six weeks each summer. The winery, office building, and apartment building were all part of the same complex. We had apartments on the fourth floor, visiting relatives stayed in the two apartments on the third floor, and the second floor housed our offices. The bottling line occupied the first floor, and the lower level housed the oak tanks that aged the wines.

Billy and Johnny loved their vacations there. The winery was their playground. Once, one of the winery hands put Johnny on the conveyor belt with the wine bottles; he laughed with delight as he went around the bottling line. (It wasn't quite as funny the time the same fellow put him on a forklift and let him drive it around the winery. He was only inches away from a wall when I shouted, "Put your foot on the brake!" He managed to stop it just before slamming into the wall.)

Both boys learned to catch fish in the stream behind the winery, and they played in the town square just across the street from the winery compound. They played soccer with the kids in town around their age and visited the town's *gelateria* (ice cream shop) down the street.

They also learned some Italian while playing with the local kids, got a firsthand look at wine making, and developed a taste for European traditions. On one of their visits, in the summer of 1967, my father-in-law took the whole family to a palatial hotel and spa in Abano. Dinners in the hotel's beautiful dining room were feasts. During one lavish dinner, Billy and Johnny, eight and seven years old respectively and already food savvy, learned the art of removing the skin of a ripe peach in one piece with the dull side of a knife.

―――――――

The 1960s brought great cultural and social change to America, and the foods and beverages Americans consumed changed dramatically as well. People who'd never even thought about drinking wine were tasting—and buying. In 1968, sales of dry table wines surpassed those of sweet fortified wines for the first time. As Americans became more and more interested in premium table wines, they chose European (usually French) brands. Even though people on the West Coast were aware that some good wines were being made in Napa and Sonoma, most still believed French wines were the best. In Chicago, I knew our success and our future were in importing fine wines. My heart said France, but I left my options open.

PENNE WITH COGNAC

Although Cheddar cheese and Cognac are not exactly staples of the Italian table, I have always liked to experiment with pasta sauces, especially when JoJo and I are cooking in the kitchen together. We open a bottle of wine while we do the prep work and then let the meal evolve. In this recipe, as in many others, bacon is the secret ingredient.

SERVES 8

4 slices thick-cut hardwood smoked bacon, diagonally sliced, divided

3 tablespoons extra-virgin olive oil

1 medium onion, chopped

Pinch of red pepper

1 can (28-ounce) Italian plum tomatoes

Salt and pepper, to taste

Bay leaf

⅓ cup good-quality Cognac

1 pound penne pasta

Hot sauce, to taste

1 cup aged white Cheddar cheese, grated

½ cup heavy cream or half and half (room temperature)

1. Cook two strips of the bacon. Set aside.

2. In large sauté pan, sauté remaining bacon with onion for about 4 minutes (do not burn onion). Add pinch of red pepper.

3. Remove stems and core of tomatoes quartered and add to pan. Season with salt, pepper, and the bay leaf. Cook over medium heat, stirring from time to time, for about 25 minutes.

4. When sauce is cooked, remove the bay leaf and pass through a

food mill. Add the Cognac, return to the sauté pan, and bring to a simmer.

5. In a pasta pot, cook the penne pasta according to directions on the box, drain, and return to the pot. Pour the sauce over the pasta in the pot. Add the hot sauce and half the Cheddar cheese, and toss until well mixed. Add the cream and toss again. The sauce should not drown the pasta.

6. Serve in pasta bowls dusted with the remaining cheddar cheese and garnished with bacon.

SUGGESTED WINES

Olvena "Cuatro 4," Chimney Rock Elevage

Steak with Mustard-Cognac Sauce

Because robust red wines are particularly pleasing to me, I enjoy preparing steak dishes to accompany them. This variation on beef Stroganoff slowly evolved when I discovered that simply saucing the steaks with the mustard-Cognac sauce was a nice variation on a theme. Sautéed mushrooms and sautéed rapini are good side dishes to serve with this entrée.

Serves 6

6 7–8 ounce steaks of choice

Salt and pepper, to taste

3 tablespoons canola oil

6 tablespoons butter, divided in half

4 cloves garlic, smashed

2 sprigs thyme, fresh

2 sprigs rosemary, freshly ground

¾ cup shallots, finely chopped

4 ounces Cognac

2 tablespoons tawny Port

2 cups chicken broth, room temperature

2 tablespoons Dijon mustard

1. Preheat the oven to 250°F. Sprinkle steaks on all sides with salt and pepper.

2. Heat oil in a heavy skillet over high heat. Insert steaks and sear them until brown, about 2 minutes on each side.

3. Reduce heat to medium-low and add 3 tablespoons butter, garlic, thyme, and rosemary, and cook about 10 minutes, basting with pan juices.

4. Transfer steaks to a baking sheet and keep warm in the oven.

5. Pour contents of the skillet into a bowl and return about 3 tablespoons of the sauce to the skillet. Raise the heat to high, add shallots, and sauté for 2 minutes. Add the Cognac and Port, stirring and scraping the skillet. Add the broth and bring the mixture to a boil. Allow the sauce to cook until it is reduced by half.

6. Whisk in the Dijon mustard and the remaining 3 tablespoons of butter. Season with salt and pepper and remove from heat.

7. Arrange steaks on plates, spoon over sauce, and serve.

SUGGESTED WINES

Chapoutier Hermitage "M. de La Sizeranne" Rouge, Terlato Family Vineyards Angels' Peak

Good Sports

THE QUALITY OF A PERSON'S LIFE IS IN DIRECT PROPORTION TO THEIR
COMMITMENT TO EXCELLENCE, REGARDLESS OF THEIR CHOSEN FIELD
OF ENDEAVOR.

—Vince Lombardi

THE 1960S WERE ALSO A TIME OF GREAT CHANGE IN my own private world. After Johnny's birth, we bought our first home in Sauganash, a Chicago neighborhood that bordered Lincolnwood. It was a pleasant, tree-lined community about a half mile from my in-laws' home in Lincolnwood Towers, and there were numerous good schools nearby. I had grown up knowing my grandparents, and now our boys had the advantage of growing up surrounded by their grandparents and great-grandparents as well! Just as my grandparents and parents would drop everything if I said, "I want to go outside and fly a kite," our sons' grandparents would drop everything they were doing to join in their fun. Everything revolved around whatever the grandchildren wanted to do.

The boys were lucky enough to grow up knowing four of their great-grandparents. JoJo's grandparents lived in Chicago as well, and my father's mother, Catherine Terlato, lived in an apartment close to my parents' home. My Nonna Giarrusso, my mother's mother, continued to live with my parents as she had when I was a child. Although it was becoming harder for her to get around, she would often call the boys over to her, hold them for a moment, and kiss their faces. Just as she'd called me *principe mio*, she'd call our boys the "little princes" and told them often how much she loved them. Our boys fondly remember such moments with their grandparents, and it helped shape their character in a very positive way.

The Terlato and Paterno families were a study in contrasts. My parents worked together in the liquor store and spent practically all of their time together, and they were loving and indulgent toward our sons. JoJo's parents led more independent lives. JoJo's father worked all day at Pacific Wine, and her mother, Lena, worked all day managing the family's liquor store and pizzeria. When she wasn't working, Lena was always planning something. This meant cooking, sewing, or organizing a shower, wedding, or a baptism with her many women friends. The Paternos were the godparents of virtually every child whose parents knew them! Most Friday nights, we'd all join them at their home for dinner, and there was always a flurry of activity in their house. They had five grandchildren and were particularly indulgent of their deceased son John's children, but they had plenty of love left over for our boys, especially when they all vacationed together in Italy.

I was busy, too. I traveled a lot, so JoJo's steady hand was at the wheel when it came to raising our sons. In 1964, Billy began kindergarten, and JoJo became active in the PTA. She was always the first to organize bake sales for one cause or another at the school or substitute as a teacher's aide whenever needed. When Johnny started kindergarten a year later, she was the one who went with him, distracting him from his tears, holding his hand, and reassuring him that school would be fun.

Weekends were my time with the boys. On Saturdays, we made breakfast together—eggs, toast, and sausage or ham. Billy liked his eggs basted, so after a short lifetime of eating them over easy, he finally told JoJo, "I think I'd like to make them myself. I don't like the eggs turned over." All by himself, he'd figured out how to baste them by spooning hot butter over the yolks. A few years later, Johnny, who loved eggs Benedict, began experimenting with the dish himself. Whenever we ate breakfast in restaurants, he'd always compare their eggs Benedict to his—and his usually came out on top. I encouraged the boys to venture into our garden to pick basil, rosemary, parsley, and tomatoes from the vine and add them to a dish of scrambled eggs or pasta to learn about differences in flavor and, eventually, train their palates. I suppose cooking and tasting just came naturally to them, given our family traditions, but it was also a sign of what was to come. The boys were gaining the confidence to think for themselves, and they could tell the difference between a well-made dish and one that wasn't.

Both of my sons were comfortable around adults from a very young age, and they were used to being with what some would consider to be highly successful people—sports figures, famous chefs, winemakers from all parts of the world, and people in the media. Both boys were taught to be seen more than heard. They knew how to sit at a table properly and not fidget or act up, and they respected the adults they encountered.

They also respected each other. I'd witnessed so many disputes in other families that had left siblings sharply divided, so early on, I told them, "You can fight with someone else, if necessary, but you can never fight with each other." I made them vow to always respect one another and look out for each other's family in the future. To this day, they have never disappointed me.

Our family didn't put too much stock in make-believe. We didn't talk about the Easter Bunny bringing gifts, or the Tooth Fairy putting coins under their pillows. For a while, they did believe their Christmas gifts came from Santa Claus, but their older cousins soon set them straight about the little old man with white whiskers. Whenever they asked a question, JoJo and I would answer them as honestly as we could.

One of my biggest thrills was introducing our boys to the sports I had enjoyed as a kid and continued to play as an adult. On Saturdays, I took Billy and Johnny to the Illinois Athletic Club, where I played handball with my friends Guy Armanetti and Chicago Cubs third baseman Ron Santo. The boys worked out with me, and I taught them to play handball.

In 1965, I began my seven-year career as a baseball coach at Shabonna Park on Chicago's northwest side, where the boys' baseball career spanned from the Peewee League to the Pony League. It was the first competitive sports experience the boys had, and I made sure they learned discipline, tenacity, confidence, teamwork, and good sportsmanship, as well as the need for endless practice. The baseball program was a valuable experience for our sons and all the other boys who participated on the team.

I started coaching the team when the former coach was transferred out of state. At the end of the first half of the season, the point where I'd started coaching them, their record was 0–7. I renamed the team Paterno Imports, kept all of the same players, and by the end of the second half of the season, the team's record was 7–7.

All of the games were played on Saturday and Sunday, and the kids practiced twice a week, Tuesdays and Thursdays, starting immediately after school. I required them to practice from three o'clock until dusk, when we couldn't see the ball anymore. The kids loved it. On many nights, parents came to watch the last hour or two of practice.

I taught the players how to run bases, do rundowns, straddle a base when putting down a tag, follow the ball after it was hit, slide, and cut off throws from the outfield. Of course, I taught them to never take a walk. I wanted them to know that the purpose of the game was to hit the ball. They had to have the confidence to hit and not be ashamed to strike out. They learned how to look and act like ball players. Their uniforms had to be washed for each game, and no one was allowed to wear his hat any way except the way it was intended. Paterno Imports had the best-looking team in our league, which I believe helped their confidence.

I never had problems with parents, because every kid played and contributed what he could. At the end of each game, my players were obliged to cross the field to the other team's bench, shake hands with the players, and wish them well in their following games. We didn't lose a game in three years. At the last award dinner, their trophies were presented by Ron Santo, Pete Rose, Ernie Banks, and boxing legend Tony Zale.

Ron Santo always said that if you work hard, you have to play hard. As I got older, I enjoyed playing golf and found riding horses to be very relaxing. I bought my first horse, a palomino, and boarded it at a stable on Cumberland Road near Lawrence Avenue with access to riding trails that led all the way into Wisconsin. Santo boarded his horse at the same stable, as did some of my other friends. I spent many evenings on the trails as the sun set. Many Saturday mornings, my sons and I would meet friends for breakfast and spend the rest of the day riding. Both boys took to the saddle quickly. One of our quarter horses, Redigo Bar, was particularly smart. He quickly sensed the boys' youth and inexperience. Their feet couldn't reach the stirrups, so riding was as dangerous as bareback for them. No matter how much their little feet would urge him to go faster, he'd never leave the gentle gait that prevented them from falling off.

It was a great way to spend Saturday mornings, and even JoJo learned to ride. She showed up with a friend, Anna Marie Massey, at the stable one day, jumped on Redigo Bar, and rode him around the corral. Anna Marie's husband, Ralph, and I had no idea that our wives had been taking riding lessons at another stable without ever letting us know.

The boys and I continued to ride for a few years, and then golf took over. I bought Billy and Johnny a set of golf clubs and lessons at Brookwood Country Club. Billy hit endless buckets of balls on the range and showed promise. Johnny loved it too, but his enthusiasm was split between golf and trapshooting. Ron Santo had been right—the intensity of work had to match the intensity of play.

During the boys' grammar school years, I was more actively engaged in Pacific Wine Company's distribution business, and my father-in-law headed up Paterno Imports. Although we traveled to Italy together on important trips, I spent most of my time in Chicago, worked on various fundraising events with my father-in-law, and supported many political candidates and community organizations, such as Congressman Frank Annunzio's Youth for Old Age program, which enlisted the help of successful Italian-American Chicagoans, and others to benefit Villa Scalabrini, a retirement home for elderly Italians in Melrose Park.

Such associations led to close friendships and even led me to an interesting pizza venture. In 1967, Gene Pullano, an insurance salesman; Ron Mayer, a tailor; Lou Bonelli, owner of the pizzeria Il Forno; Ron Santo; and I decided to go into the carryout pizza franchise business. Santo came up with the pizza idea himself. He'd ordered a pizza delivered to his home in suburban Park Ridge. After a few bites, he threw it out and said he could make a better pizza himself. Soon after that incident, we opened a Ron Santo's Pizza in Park Ridge and got involved in franchises. We put ovens in the Wrigley Field commissary and sold 50,000 individual-sized pies in half a season. The pizza, packaged as "The Pro's Pizza," featured a photo of a Cubs player on each box. Next, we ventured into the retail market, selling seven-inch pies two to a box (we called it the "Doubleheader").

For a while, things went so well that we bought the printing company that supplied the menus. We opened two franchise stores in addition to the one we owned. Unfortunately, we were all involved in growing our own businesses and simply didn't have enough time to dedicate to the venture. The general manager we hired didn't have the expertise to take it forward, so we removed the Ron Santo name and sold the operation. Fortunately, it was a good experience overall, and we all remained good friends.

JoJo also had her own entrepreneurial endeavors. With her mother and sister, she started a jewelry and accessory business for the benefit of their friends and acquaintances. On their various trips to Italy, they scouted out fine jewelers who took orders for rings, bracelets, brooches, and pins. They showed the jewelry privately by appointment, and the business was quite successful. Word spread, and they extended their offerings to include designer scarves and other accessories.

No matter how much we were involved with our business ventures, though, the yearly family vacation always took precedence. My vote was usually for Florida. My in-laws had a winter vacation home near Fort Lauderdale, and whether we went to Disney World in Orlando or some other part of Florida first, we always visited them before returning Chicago. In 1974, my father-in-law suffered a minor stroke and started to have other related health problems, so we frequently combined business with our vacation visit because I could go over the financials and other business matters with him.

Billy enrolled in Loyola Academy in 1973, and Johnny followed the next year. The boys' high school years coincided with the years I became more and more involved with Paterno Imports, but I still tried to go to all of Billy's basketball games and Johnny's football games. I loved watching them play, because I knew they would have to compete with others for the rest of their lives. The lessons they learned on courts and on fields would serve them well in the future. But at the same time, JoJo and I always drummed into their heads that as much as they loved to compete with others, they should never compete with each other.

I set standards and expected Billy and Johnny to follow them, especially during their high school years. If they had any ideas about veering from the straight and narrow, I wouldn't give them the chance. I wouldn't go to sleep at night until they came home, and the use of the car was always a tug of war. Just before his high school graduation, Billy was grounded for a week for an infraction.

JoJo said more than once that if we'd had a daughter, she would have left the house at sixteen—no young girl would have lived in the house under my rules. I may not have been easy, but I was fair, and the boys knew that I meant what I said. Today, they are raising their children the same way.

When the boys took jobs at the business during summer

vacations, I told them, "You must arrive before me in the morning, and leave after me in the evening." It didn't give me pleasure to be hard on them, but I wanted to make sure that everyone in the company respected them. _____

In their last years in high school and first years of college, Billy and Johnny spent quite a bit of time with school friends Michael and Tony Lazzaroni whose parents had a home on Lake Geneva, Wisconsin, a popular weekend escape for Chicagoans. There, they fell in love with waterskiing. JoJo knew the boys' parents, Cory and Toni Lazzaroni, very well, and we were frequently invited to join the family for weekends at the lake. Over time, we developed a very close friendship with them and began spending almost every weekend at their home on the lake. Around the same time, a Playboy Club opened nearby with an excellent golf course. The course was a compelling draw for me, and I suppose other aspects of the club appealed to the boys as well.

When a condominium became available in Geneva Towers in 1980, we purchased it. Lake Geneva was about fifty miles from our Sauganash home—an easy commute on a Friday afternoon—and we enjoyed our weekends at the lake all summer long. Although Billy had enrolled in Chicago's Loyola University in 1978, he made the trip out to Lake Geneva to join us each weekend.

Waterskiing was a fun diversion for everyone except JoJo, who was terribly afraid of the water. After months of coaching, including standing alongside her in the pool in waist-high water, she gained the confidence she needed that the ski vest would keep her afloat. Little by little, we moved toward the deep end until her feet couldn't touch the bottom. Once she was satisfied that the vest worked, she was ready to give waterskiing a try, but it took many attempts—and Cory Lazzaroni's infinite patience—before she and the skis stayed on top of the water. She gradually built up the courage to slalom on one ski around the lake (an impressive seventeen miles), but to this day she remains afraid of water and still can't swim. As our family's passion for waterskiing developed, we bought a boat and enjoyed countless days together in the sun.

Meanwhile, a catastrophic 1973 fire nearly destroyed Leading Liquor Marts, and my parents had decided not to rebuild. When another condominium became available at Geneva Towers, they purchased it and joined us at the lake each weekend.

Johnny was the first of the boys to leave home, entering the architecture program at Arizona State in 1979. For JoJo, it felt just like the first day the boys went off to grammar school; she hated the idea of Johnny leaving home. I felt differently; I was proud that he was taking steps to make it on his own. I warmly accepted Johnny's decision. Over the years, I'd seen many scions coast through college straight into waiting jobs at their father's companies. I had always preached that our sons should maintain good grades, get their degrees, and look for work elsewhere. Furthermore, I told them often that they probably wouldn't like working with me, and that doing so might spoil the wonderful family unity we had. (I really didn't mean it, of course, but it sounded good at the time.)

Meanwhile, JoJo and I began to enjoy our own private getaways. Each winter, we traveled to the Caribbean island of St. Martin with friends who knew the island well and shared our passion for waterskiing. We stayed at Mullet Bay on the island's Dutch side, but the food and wine on the French side of the island eventually lured us to the great accommodations and memorable meals of La Samanna resort. JoJo loved to shop in the arcades off the cobblestone streets of the French side's capital city, Marigot, for jewelry, clothes, and French porcelain. I was drawn to Marigot's musty wine cellars and countless bottles of important Bordeaux wines and fine Cuban cigars, both of which the French merchants had in abundance.

Even during these island escapes, I always wondered what my next step would be. I was always thinking about new ways to grow the business, ways I'd never thought of before.

CHIVE RISOTTO WITH TRUFFLE OIL

The versatility of that great Italian standby, risotto, is very appealing because so many different ingredients can be used. We've found that a risotto with truffles for our very special Renaissance Club Truffle Dinner was the sine qua non *for the ultimate risotto recipe. It's very special.*

SERVES 6

1 cup quartered chives

1 cup parsley leaves, loosely packed

1 tablespoon olive oil

2 tablespoons butter

⅓ cup onion, minced

1½ cups carnaroli rice

¼ cup white wine

5 cups chicken broth

1 cup grated fresh Parmigiano-Reggiano cheese, divided

1 tablespoon butter, softened

1 tablespoon truffle butter

1 tablespoon white truffle oil, plus 1 tablespoon for garnish

1 small black truffle, shaved

Salt and pepper, to taste

1. In a small pot of boiling salted water, cook chives and parsley for 15 to 20 seconds. Drain in a colander and submerge in ice water. Pat the herbs dry and mince.

2. In a risotto pan over medium heat, warm the 2 tablespoons butter and olive oil. Add onion, stirring (be sure you do not burn the onion). Add the rice and stir until completely coated.

3. Add the wine and continue stirring. After most of the wine has been absorbed, begin adding the broth, 1 cup at a time, until all the broth is absorbed, approximately 16 minutes. Stir continuously to prevent the rice from sticking to the pan.

4. After the rice has been cooking approximately 16 minutes, stir in herbs, ½ cup Parmigiano-Reggiano cheese, the 1 tablespoon of softened butter, some salt and pepper, and 1 tablespoon of truffle oil. Stir for 1 minute or so and then add remaining truffle oil.

5. Serve in bowls and garnish with shaved black truffle.

SUGGESTED WINES
Santa Margherita Luna dei Feldi, Maurizio Zanella Chardonnay

Filet Mignon Diane

Great beef and great wine are my recipe for a celebration. While traditional Diane recipes use a cut of sirloin, I use beef fillets and serve them with a bottle of Domaine Terlato & Chapoutier Malakoff Shiraz or, if I'm really celebrating, a bottle of EPISODE.

Serves 4

Fillets:

4 6-ounce beef fillets

1 tablespoon olive oil

1 tablespoon crushed fresh black peppercorns

1½ teaspoons sea salt

Sauce:

1 tablespoon butter

1 tablespoon finely minced shallots

¾ cup dry red wine

½ tablespoon balsamic vinegar

1 tablespoon Dijon mustard

1 teaspoon Worcestershire sauce

1 cup demi-glace

3 tablespoons Cognac

1 teaspoon tomato paste

2 tablespoons heavy cream

Salt and pepper, to taste

1. Melt the butter in a saucepan, and sauté the shallots 3 to 4 minutes, until wilted.

2. Add wine, vinegar, Worcestershire sauce, and tomato paste and reduce until almost dry. Add mustard and demi-glace, and stir until mixed. Increase heat to high, add cognac, and flame.

3. Lower the heat to a simmer and reduce by half. Add heavy cream and reduce until slightly thickened. Season to taste. Keep warm.

4. Rub fillets with olive oil on all sides, mix pepper and salt together, and press on surfaces of fillets.

5. Cook fillets on a hot grill or in a cast iron frying pan for 8 to 9 minutes on one side and 5 minutes on the other side, to desired degree of doneness.

6. Serve either whole or sliced, with sauce.

SUGGESTED WINES
Château des Laurets, Chanson Beaune Clos des Mouches Red, Ernie Els Cirrus Syrah

PART III

[1978—1981]

It's All in the Name

LEADERSHIP IS THE ABILITY TO RECOGNIZE A PROBLEM BEFORE IT BECOMES
AN EMERGENCY.

—Napoleon Bonaparte

I N 1972, I WAS DINING WITH GUESTS AT TRIMANI, A restaurant in the Ghetto neighborhood of Rome, when I noticed that a wine with a green label was being served at a number of nearby tables. I asked our waiter about the wine, and he responded, "It's Corvo, a dry white wine made from Inzolia grapes. It comes from Sicily."

Never one to pass up a popular restaurant wine, I ordered a bottle. My guests and I drank glass after glass of the Corvo and ate and talked about food and business as the time flew by. When the waiter gave me the check at the end of the evening, I was shocked to find a charge for four bottles of wine. How could we have consumed four bottles, I wondered? I asked the waiter if it was possible that the checks had been mixed up.

"No, you drank four bottles of wine, including the first bottle you ordered. You even surprised me," he told me.

"My God, this wine is so easy to drink!" I thought. The next day, I called Corvo, which was owned by the Region of Sicily, an entity that was an arm of the Sicilian government. I reached a company representative named Letto and told him, "I saw your wine at a restaurant in Rome, tasted it, and absolutely love it. Do you have an agent in the United States?"

Letto confirmed that they did. In those days, agent contracts generally lasted no more than two or three years, because no supplier wanted to "get married" for very long.

I replied, "My name is Anthony Terlato, and I represent Gancia in the United States. When you are ready to leave your importer, let me know. I am very interested."

Letto answered, "Right now, we're happy with our importer. We're doing 1,146 cases in the United States."

"We could sell that much in just a suburb of Chicago," I responded.

Letto paused. "Give me your name and address. If we think about making a change, I'll call you."

I figured that was the end of it, but about four or five months later, Letto called. He was in New York and wanted to visit me in Chicago. I immediately invited him to join our family for dinner at our home.

That was our manner of doing business, and JoJo was a wonderful hostess, just as her mother was for her father. Paterno Imports was a family business built on a concept of hospitality. I brought clients, business associates, and friends into my home and into my kitchen. To me, it was crucial to open a bottle of wine and visit informally over a home-cooked meal before getting down to serious business.

Over a dinner of three-cheese risotto and lamb loin matched with good wine, we began to talk. Letto told me that Corvo had become unhappy with its importer. "He only has a small business in New York," he said. "He has no reach. You're selling Gancia throughout the United States, and we think we'd like to work with you."

I was thrilled. Corvo's history goes all the way back to 1824. The Duca of Salaparuta, a Sicilian nobleman, took the Grand Tour in that year. He spent many months studying and drinking great wines in France, talking with winemakers and scholars, and appreciating all of the art, music, and literature that the Continent offered. Afterward, he returned to his ancestral home on the northern shore of the island with an ambition to create a winery and estate that would be the talk of Italy. To realize his dream, he brought Chardonnay cuttings back with him and hired a few French enologists, German technicians, and Italian viticulturists to make it happen. With their help, he created an unrivaled winery in the small seaside village of Casteldaccia and named his wines *Corvo* (Italian for crow) in honor of a local legend about the crows that nested on the turrets of his castle. He married a very beautiful woman who was related to the king, and they became the aristocracy of Sicily. After the duke died, his winery fell into decline, and eventually the Region of Sicily bought it.

Other Italian wines, such as Bolla Soave, Frascati, and Verdicchio, were selling for $3.98 a bottle at the time. Corvo was the first Italian wine to surpass the $4.00-per-bottle price range and build to a significant volume. I knew Corvo was a good wine with an interesting bit of history.

We asked the Sicilian government for a ten-year contract, and they negotiated some really high numbers. I couldn't imagine how we were going to sell it, but there was no way I wasn't going to try. I committed to sell 6,000 cases in the first year and landed the ten-year contract. After all, the worst thing that could happen was that we would lose the brand if we didn't perform.

When my father-in-law and I visited Sicily a short time later, we realized that we would need a local attorney to draw up the contract. One of Paterno's friends recommended Magistrato Tannino LoCoco, a Palermo-based attorney who was also the head of the Criminal Division of the Supreme Court of Appeals in Rome. We got in touch with him and invited him to dinner.

We were delighted to discover that LoCoco, a well-dressed,

impeccably mannered gentleman, was also a true gourmet. I'd never met such a knowledgable, gracious, and humble man, and I was deferential to him in every way. As we left the restaurant, I said, "After you."

He replied, "No, after you. You have to go first."

"No, you're much more important. You have to go through the door first," I said.

He smiled and settled the issue by saying, "If you heard the way my wife talked to me, you wouldn't think I'm more important than anyone."

With LoCoco's contract in hand, we met with Corvo's manager and signed on the dotted line.

In the early 1970s, we had four district managers working for us at Paterno Imports, and each had a corner of the country to service. Needless to say, they had their hands full. During that period, my father-in-law's health was becoming more and more of an issue, so we decided to enlist some help. We arranged for Heublein, a spirits and food distributor, to be the United States agent for all of Paterno's agency brands. The Connecticut-based company agreed to pay us $1 million a year, no matter how many cases they sold. A million a year was much more than we were making, so it was a great deal.

However, much to my surprise, Neil Bianchini, Heublein's manager of imported wines, told us, "We don't want Corvo. There is no market in the United States for Sicilian white wines."

Disbelieving, I replied, "We're disbanding our import company, giving you all the brands, and you're not taking Corvo? We have a contract with Corvo. Who's going to sell it?"

Bianchini shrugged. "See what you can do with it. We're not interested."

As a first step, I took Corvo to the restaurants, because many waiters in the United States—especially in New York—were Italian. To them, Corvo was a patriotic symbol of Italy. The waiters immediately recognized the wine, and Corvo immediately began to sell well in neighborhood Italian restaurants.

I also ran a Corvo radio commercial in the New York market. I went to the Italian radio stations first and eventually moved on to the English-speaking stations. The commercials captured a lot of attention, and Corvo started to catch on.

I also worked with the restaurants directly. I liked to make my calls around one thirty, just as the lunch hour was winding down. I'd visit each restaurant with a chilled bottle of Corvo concealed in a small bag, sit down at a table by myself, order a dish of pasta, and tell the waiter, "I'd like to have a bottle of Corvo white, please." If the waiter replied, "We don't carry that wine," I'd ask to see the restaurant's owner.

Next, I'd ask the owner if he'd ever heard of Corvo. No matter what his response might be, I'd pull out the bottle and invite him to have a glass with me. I would explain to the owner that I planned to get a distributor in New York, but first, I wanted to line up a number of restaurant orders just in case the distributor was hesitant about handling a Sicilian white wine.

I stayed in New York for three days, visited fifteen to twenty restaurants, and wrote orders for more than 250 cases. On the last day, I met with the New York distributor and proudly showed him my list of restaurant orders. He promptly bought a 600-case container. After conquering New York, I also built a strong restaurant business for Corvo in New Jersey, Detroit, St. Louis, and, of course, Chicago.

Over the next four years, we sold more Corvo than Heublein had sold of all our agency wines combined. Heublein excelled at marketing spirits, but the company just didn't understand the imported wine businesss. Although Heublein paid us the same sum every year, our wines didn't move, and the brands were stagnant. When Paterno and I saw Heublein's management at the next annual meeting, we told them our brands were dying.

One of the managers, an accountant, retorted, "What do you care? You're getting $1 million a year for the next seven years."

Paterno stared him down. He replied coldly, "I don't want my son-in-law to have money. I want him to have work." He removed the contract from his briefcase, tore it in half, and threw it on the table.

On our way out, I said, "What are your plans now?"

"You're my plans. Work it out."

His words were prophetic. My father-in-law was now spending more and more time at his home in Florida, so in 1977, he made me president of Paterno Imports. In addition to Pacific Wine Company, Paterno Imports was now my responsibility.

Although Paterno was clearly planning for the future, none of us was fully prepared for his death in 1978. We grieved for him. We'd lost a father and a grandfather, and I had also lost a powerful ally. The Italian community of Chicago also felt his loss. He was a major contributor to the political campaigns of many Italian office seekers, sat on the boards of many charitable organizations, and generously supported the Italian senior home, Villa Scalabrini.

Soon after Paterno's death, I went to Italy to reassure our suppliers that Paterno Imports would continue to market their wines. I started with Vittorio Gancia, our oldest supplier and one of my father-in-law's closest friends. We talked about my father-in-law and the business. Toward the end of our visit, Gancia said,

"Tony, do you want to be just another importer of French wine, or would you like to become the most important importer of Italian wine in the United States?"

Gancia's words rang in my ears all night. After my return to Chicago, I called him and said, "I need to know more about Italian wines."

"Next time you come to Italy," he offered, "I'll take you to visit some of the most important wineries. Without my introduction, it would be hard for you to get your foot in the door. I will help you." It was an invitation as well as a challenge, and because I was now responsible for both Paterno Imports and Pacific Wine, I hustled back to Italy as soon as I could.

During the late 1970s and early 1980s, I spent three months a year in Italy, using the home in Greve-in-Chianti as my base. I remember some of those trips as if they were yesterday, and one 1975 trip looms particularly large in my memory. Mario Cortevesio, our winemaker at Mirafiore, was a *maestro assaggitore* (master taster)—one of only seven in all of Italy at the time. I was looking for a Brunello di Montalcino for our portfolio, so Cortevesio and I drove to Montalcino. We visited four or five restaurants, and at each we ordered a dish of pasta and five or six Brunellos from the wine list. After tasting about twenty different wines, we determined that Il Poggione was the best of the group.

The restaurant's owner gave us directions to the winery, which was only a few miles away. Just as Cortevesio and I arrived, the heavens opened and rain began to pour. We rang the doorbell and were greeted by a well-dressed gentleman.

"How can I help you?"

Standing in the freezing rain, I shivered and told him I was an American importer interested in Il Poggione.

He responded, "We are not interested in selling our wine in the United States."

As he spoke, a voice piped up from inside the house. "Piero, who is it? Invite him in. It is raining." The voice belonged to Clemente Franceschi, the winery's seventy-seven-year-old owner. Franceschi was perched in a wheelchair before a roaring fire; alas, the fire did little to temper the cold. "Piero" turned out to be Piero Talenti, Il Poggione's *fattore* (winemaker and estate manager).

It was early evening, so Franceschi asked if we had eaten. Even though we'd both already downed four dishes of pasta each that afternoon, I replied, "No." I realized Franceschi was going to offer something, and I wanted the opportunity to speak with him.

Despite Franceschi's hospitality, in the first twenty minutes Talenti reiterated at least a half-dozen times, loud and clear, that he wasn't interested in selling in the United States.

We spent a few hours discussing everything from weather to grape growing while tasting several Brunello vintages with crispy bread, prosciutto, cheese, and olives. Finally, Franceschi turned to Talenti and said, "*Fattore*, give this man some wine for the United States."

Needless to say, Talenti was taken aback—and so was I. But the look on Franceschi's face made his message clear. He cleared his throat and spoke. "Young man, I'm giving you the wine because you have been here for three hours and never once asked for the price."

Cortevesio and I left Montalcino very happy. Over the years I visited Il Poggione frequently, and Talenti and I became very close. A few years later, Clemente Franceschi passed away and his son, Leopoldo (a true gentleman's gentleman), became the proprietor of Il Poggione. The younger Franceschi is much like his father, and today Il Poggione is known for its quality more than ever before.

From my base in Greve-in-Chianti, I also made frequent jaunts north to Piedmont and south to Sicily, but I stopped in Tuscany more than any other area because so much of our business was centered there. The routine was always the same—I'd hop off a plane, leap into a rental car, and run around to various wineries. There was no such thing as e-mail or cellular phones in that day, so communication with my secretary in Chicago was out of the question. I worked on my proposals in the evening and made winery calls during the day.

After my father-in-law passed away, I realized that I needed a strong, experienced, financially minded person to keep me balanced. John Scribner was a partner in the accounting firm we worked with. I asked his partners if I could have him work with me exclusively for a year—that is, if he was willing. Apparently, they didn't want to lose him, so they told me I couldn't afford him.

When I had my first meeting with the bank after my father-in-law's death, Scribner came with me, and I could see he spoke the bankers' language well. On our way back to the office, I told him what his partners had said and asked if it was true that I couldn't afford him. Surprised, he said, "Absolutely not!" He did say that if I was serious about bringing him on, he would need a contract before he could negotiate his buyout from the firm.

A week later, Scribner brought me a ten-page working agreement and asked me to take it home and read it. Relieved, I turned to the last page and immediately signed it.

Scribner was shocked. He said, "The agreement lists the salary I require, the car I need, and the vacation time I want."

I told him that I didn't need to read it. "I trust you."

He tore up the agreement and said, "I guess I don't need a contract with you."

Now that I had someone I could trust to watch the money, I could concentrate on growing our sales. Scribner was also a valuable ally in other ways. He often accompanied me on my trips to Italy to help out with the inherent contract issues that would come up.

The idea of supporting an Italian bank had always appealed to Paterno, so when the Banco di Roma opened a branch in Chicago in 1977, he had decided to use it as our company's primary bank, and the Central National Bank became our secondary bank. A few months after Paterno passed away, the president of Banco di Roma contacted me and requested a meeting. Because Paterno had always managed the bank relationships, I really didn't know what to expect.

The meeting was brief and to the point: He wanted to know what personal security I could put up to back the loan my father-in-law had negotiated. Surprised, I told him I was unaware that we had ever posted any personal security before.

"Well," he said, "we knew Tony Paterno very well," implying that now, things were different.

I asked what he would consider as "security."

"Your home would be fine," he answered.

I left without further comment, remembering something my father had told me years before: "Don't ever put up your home as security for anything, because it can hurt your wife and children."

Needless to say, I didn't care for Banco di Roma's high-handed way of doing business. I walked across the street and asked to see Jackson Smart, the newly appointed chairman of the Central

National Bank. Although we had never met before, he saw me right away. I explained the situation, and he asked me to join him at Les Nomades for dinner that evening.

I learned that evening that Jack Smart was a true wine guy. He maintained a residence in Michigan and was a member of the Michigan chapters of the Commanderie de Bordeaux aux États-Unis d'Amérique, a confederation of American lovers of Bordeaux wine, and the Confrérie des Chevaliers du Tastevin, an exclusive club of Burgundy wine enthusiasts; both were organizations I belonged to in Chicago. We also discovered that we had many friends in common. We had a great dinner, drank some excellent wines, and talked for a few hours. At the end of the evening, he asked me to stop by the bank in the morning.

When we met in his office, he told me he had inquired about the amount of our loan at the Banco di Roma. He said that he would be happy to perform a wire transfer to cover our loan, if I wanted.

"From now on," Smart added, "Central National Bank will be happy to handle your financial needs, and we won't need your home as security." I walked across the street and did exactly as he had suggested. The president was in his office with two of his vice presidents; I advised him that he'd be receiving a wire transfer to pay off the loan and conveyed my gratitude for all the courtesies that the Banco di Roma had extended to my father-in-law. As I turned to leave, I registered the shock on their faces.

My banking relationship with Jack Smart evolved into a warm personal relationship that included our wives and both our sons, who he enjoyed very much. I listened to every word of advice he ever offered, including "Some guys are born on third base and think they hit a triple," and, "Run your business as if you were going to go public, and then don't." He also told me that bringing John Scribner into the business had been a very smart decision, because good salesmen need financial balance.

———————

Exciting things were happening in Italian winemaking during the 1970s and 1980s. Italian winemakers were beginning to make serious investments in their vineyards. In 1966, Piero Antinori took over his family's 600-year-old vineyard southwest of Florence, and shortly afterward, he and his winemaker, Renzo Cotarella, introduced a mixture of Sangiovese and Cabernet Sauvignon called Tignanello. Their plan was to create a new category of wine that would put Italy alongside France in the minds of consumers worldwide as a producer of premium-priced fine wines. In 1972, Angelo Gaja almost single-handedly began changing the way the wines of Barbaresco and Barolo were viewed, and he became the force behind the revolution that catapulted the wines of Piedmont to worldwide respect.

There was also a decided shift from producing bulk wines, which were either drunk at home or sent to France to be bottled and sold as *vin de pays* (wine of the region), to producing quality Italian bottled wines labeled with *denominazione d'origine controllata* (DOC) approval. Producers of premium wines were finding it difficult to meet consumer demand for their best limited-production wines. Many producers also felt hindered by the rigid DOC regulations, which stipulated, for example, that Chianti must be made from Sangiovese and no less than ten percent of white varieties, such as Trebbiano and Malvasia, and as much as twenty percent of other red varieties, such as Canaiolo. Producers such as the late Sergio Manetti of Montevertine and Fabrizio Bianchi of Monsanto were making red wines that could not legally be called Chianti because of the blend of grapes. These wines, which were often entirely Sangiovese, could only carry a legal designation of *vino da tavola* (table wine) with a geographic indication of Tuscany.

It was not until a producer with the stature and marketing clout of Antinori defied the DOC Chianti regulations with his 1971 Tignanello (not released until 1978) that Super-Tuscan wines gained critical mass. By the early 1980s, scores of other notable Chianti producers began releasing elite reds. These wines were so impressive that the humble designation *vino da tavola* became a badge of honor for Italian wines. As a result, some of Italy's best wines from the 1980s and early 1990s were designated *vino da tavola* instead of DOC.

A subtle shift in emphasis from French to Italian food and wine also occurred in the United States around the same time. It started with an intensified focus on fresh and seasonal ingredients in California and blossomed into a consumer surge of interest in whatever the latest specialty food would be—extra-virgin olive oil, aged balsamic vinegar, sun-dried tomatoes, olives, or white truffles. Wealthy Americans flocked to cooking schools in Bologna, Venice, Florence, Rome, and Sicily. Pasta *primavera* was the most popular item on the menu at Sirio Maccioni's fashionable New York restaurant, Le Cirque. Restaurants from New York City to San Francisco began to toss radicchio and arugula into their salads. Wines designated simply as "red" or "white" would soon fall out of favor—Corvo included.

Sales of the varietal wines of Piedmont and Tuscany began to take off, and I realized the great potential of bringing the higher-quality Italian wines into the States. For example, Italian winemaker Marchese Incisa della Rocchetta, a great admirer of Bordeaux wines, believed Bordelais varieties would grow better at sea level in the warmer climes of the Tuscan coast than in the cooler, hilly, and inland Chianti zone. In the mid-1960s, he created Sassicaia, a wine composed of seventy-five percent Cabernet Sauvignon and twenty-five percent Cabernet Franc. The wine didn't become commercially available until 1968 and wasn't sold worldwide until the early 1980s, when della Rocchetta's nephew, Antinori, began exporting his uncle's wines.

I felt that the well-known Italian white wines of the period, such as Orvieto, Frascati, Soave, and Verdicchio, would never sell for more than $5 a bottle, so in 1979, I returned to Italy to find a white varietal that could command a higher price in the high-end restaurants. I began my trip in Milan, where I stayed at the Palace Hotel. After many visits to the Palace, I got to know the staff very well—especially the maître d', Gaetano Crepa, who knew I was in the wine business. Crepa always made sure I was seated at a quiet corner table, since I was always writing or reading wine magazines while dining. Every evening, I would challenge him to serve me an Italian wine I didn't know. On this particular trip, I told him I had to find an absolutely spectacular white wine.

He brought me a bottle of Pinot Grigio, and it was love at first taste. When I called the winery the next morning, they told me they were too small to consider exporting their wine. Next, I called my friend Renato Ratti, who gave me the names of five excellent producers of Pinot Grigio.

I drove to Portogruaro, which coincidentally was the location of the estate winery of the Conti Marzotto, and checked into the Antico Spessotto. My room's closet was so small that I couldn't hang my jackets straight—they had to be hung on an angle. After I unpacked, I decided to walk around town and find a restaurant. I found several food stands but couldn't find a restaurant.

After wandering around for a while, I went back to the hotel and asked the clerk, "Where are all the restaurants in town?" He walked over to a pair of curtained French doors and opened them to reveal a small and beautiful restaurant, right there in the hotel. The tables were painted white and were covered with white tablecloths, and the walls were painted a dark green. The waiters wore black pants and white shirts. The place was spotless.

I ordered a dish of pasta in a simple tomato sauce with some fresh basil on top and asked for the wine list. It listed eighteen Pinot Grigios, and I ordered a bottle of each. The waiter rushed back into the kitchen and alerted the owner that something unusual was happening.

In a matter of minutes, the staff wheeled out a cloth-draped cart loaded with eighteen bottles of wine. Everyone in the restaurant stared, expecting a crowd to arrive within moments.

The owner emerged from the kitchen and asked, "When is the rest of your party coming?" It was a logical question.

"I'm alone," I told him.

He hesitated, and said, "Are you sure you want to drink all of these tonight?"

"I'm not going to drink them. I just want to taste them."

With that, he offered to taste them with me. I discovered that each wine was distinctively different. The ones that came from Friuli were very aromatic, and the ones from Trentino–Alto Adige were crisp, with a wonderful balance of acidity. Some were in Bordeaux-shaped clear bottles, and some were in tall Riesling bottles. They were all interesting, and I knew that I'd at least found the right varietal to enter the restaurant market with a wine that could handle a price point above $10.

After tasting all eighteen wines, both the restaurant's owner and I agreed that the Santa Margherita was the most interesting. He spoke highly of the owners of the winery—their commitment to quality, freshness of product, business management, and seriousness. I suddenly remembered the temperature zones Renato Ratti had shown me years before. Dead center between the two lines Ratti had drawn lay the Alto Adige, the zone where Santa Margherita Pinot Grigio was grown. Fortunately, Santa Margherita was one of the wineries I had scheduled to visit the next afternoon.

I drove past many vineyards on my way to Santa Margherita. When I arrived, I was greeted by Arrigo Marcier, the manager and export director. After a tour of the winery, I presented him with the plan I'd conceived the night before for their Pinot Grigio. Marcier asked if I would return the next day at about the same time of day, and I agreed. I went back to the hotel, confident that I had created some interest. That evening, I enjoyed another dish of pasta with my new friend at the hotel and told him about my visit.

The next day, Marcier told me our proposal was very interesting. He had contacted Vittorio Gancia and Renato Ratti to establish that our company was serious about Italian wines. Then he told me another American agent had said he would purchase three times what I'd offered to purchase in the first year.

"Would you like to make a change in your numbers?" he asked.

I replied, "What I said I would do the first year, I'll do. What they said they would do the first year, they will never do."

Marcier gave me a half smile and said, "Excuse me a minute."

Shortly after, Marcier returned and asked a number of questions about marketing, advertising, and promotion. He also wanted to know about our other wines and about the expanding wine market in the United States. The questions were friendly, and Marcier was pleased to hear that we dealt exclusively in quality wine.

He seemed satisfied and asked if I was free for dinner that night. Of course, I said yes, and he invited me to dine with him at the owner's home—Count Marzotto's palazzo, which is etched on the Santa Margherita label. I was thrilled to have the opportunity to have dinner with the count, who I later discovered was one of seven brothers whose family owned the Jolly Hotels, Hugo Boss, Marzotto fabrics, a glass company, and a milk company. The family was also poised to acquire the House of Valentino, the high-end clothing line.

I thought to myself, "The owner of the winery doesn't invite you to dinner at his home to say no." I really thought I was in the ball game at this point, so I knew it would be wise to stay relaxed and not oversell our company.

The count and I were joined that night at dinner by Marcier; the winemaker, Giorgio Mascarin; and Santa Margherita's marketing director, Fabrizio Guerrini. The palazzo's interior was even more impressive than its exterior, and it was dominated by a collection of late nineteenth-century paintings that I learned were frequently loaned to museums around the world.

Our dinner and discussion lasted several hours. I told them about my vision of Pinot Grigio ushering in the next epoch in Italian white wines in the United States, and how I thought our company could make Santa Margherita an important wine.

When I left them that night, Marcier asked me to return to the office the next day—yet another good sign. Nonetheless, I was a little nervous on my way to the winery the next morning. Marcier immediately put me at ease by telling me they had decided to give the agency to Paterno Imports. I was elated—but then he said, "I have drawn up a three-year contract for you to read."

Now I was really on the spot. Pushing my luck, I said, "I don't take on any brands for less than ten years because I can't do much in three years. I need a minimum of ten years if I am to succeed. Because I know I will succeed, I also want an option for a ten-year renewal."

"We've never done an agreement with a term that long."

"That's the only agreement I can offer you." I paused and smiled. "If you're going to get in bed with me, it's permanent. Three years is like a one-night stand."

Marcier laughed and said, "I don't think I can get that done."

I asked, "Arrigo, do you really believe in us?"

"Yes."

"Well, then, arrange it, because I won't disappoint you. I promise I will make Santa Margherita a success beyond your imagination."

"I don't know if I'm going to be able to sell that," he said. But Marcier did. He sold the count on a ten-year contract with an automatic ten-year renewal if we met the contract's goals. I cancelled all my other appointments, drove back to Milan, and took the next plane back to the States. I was excited, because I could feel that this brand had real legs. But I had a lot of work ahead of me: Although Corvo had reached 350,000 cases in sales by 1980, I was about to introduce a practically unknown varietal to the American market at a price considerably above that of any other popular Italian white wine.

As for marketing the wine in the United States, conventional wisdom dictated that we'd start on the East Coast and work west. I decided to do the opposite and start in California. I'd work my way east to New York with a success story in hand, and hopefully I'd be able to market it nationwide on television. After a year had passed, the wine surpassed our goals in California, Texas, and Chicago, and I was ready for New York.

Above—1925: My grandfather, Antonio Terlato, stands in front of his floral shop, which adjoined my father's insurance and steamship agency at 179 Hester Street, New York City.

Below—1938: Anthony Paterno's grocery store, which stood on the corner of Chicago's Grand and Western avenues.

Above—1941: My First Communion at Brooklyn's Sts. Simon & Jude Church with my cousin, Dolores Terlato Goerlich.

Below—1946: Even at twelve, I already had an appreciation for the importance of wine; here I am pictured raising a glass with cousins at a family wedding (second from the bottom on the right).

Right—1955: My father, Salvatore, and I working side-by-side in his Leading Liquor Marts, which stood at the corner of Clark Street and Ridge Avenue in Chicago.

Below—1956: Our wedding, with the happy couple at center; at left, JoJo's parents, Anthony and Lena Paterno, and at right, my parents, Frances and Salvatore Terlato.

Left—1957: My father-in-law, Anthony Paterno (right), and me at a Bolla wine tasting at Chicago's Como Inn restaurant.

Below—1961: With Alexis Lichine (right) at a tasting of the Lichine Selections' French Portfolio at Chicago's Chez Paul restaurant.

Above—1963: The legendary fourteen-hour-long lunch in the Pacific Wine Company dining room. From left: Frank Armanetti, Aaron Levin, me, Frank Schoonmaker, and Eddie Bragno.

Right—1966: Young Billy and Johnny Terlato sitting on the cornerstone of the new Pacific Wine Company building, 2701 S. Western Avenue, Chicago.

Above—1969: With Robert Mondavi at a party for the launch of his wines at Maxim's, Chicago.

Below—1970: My wonderful day as chairman of Chicago's Columbus Day Parade, alongside (clockwise from top center) Congressman Frank Annunzio, Mayor Richard J. Daley, Johnny, and Billy.

Right—1979: The television-commercial reenactment of my discovery of Santa Margherita Pinot Grigio in Portogruaro, Italy.

Center—1979: Demonstrating Renato Ratti's wine zones of Europe map.

Bottom—1984: With JoJo, celebrating Debbie and Bill's wedding.

Above—From left, Bill; Christian Moueix, owner of Château Pétrus; and John Kournetas at lunch at Pacific Wine Company.

Below—Preparing New York strip steaks with (from left) Chef Jean Joho and Count Alexandre de Lur-Saluces, owner of Château d'Yquem.

Right top—2000: Dining with Julia Child at the American Institute of Wine & Food Annual Benefit.

Right center— With Baroness Philippine de Rothschild at a party for the launch of Mouton-Cadet at Pacific Wine Company.

Below—1998: Preparing dinner at Tangley Oaks with (from left) Felidia's Executive Chef Fortunato Nicotra, Lidia Bastianich, and Colin Crowley.

Above—With (from left) John, Marvin Shanken of *Wine Spectator*, and Bill at a four-man golf outing.

Below—With (from left) Joey Mondelli, Victor Skrebneski, and John at Mondelli's La Scarola restaurant in Chicago.

Above—Celebrating a golf win at Gianotti's with (from left) Vic Gianotti, Doc Daddono, and Ralph Massey.

Below—At the annual truffle dinner with Chef Paul Bartolotta, holding a white truffle.

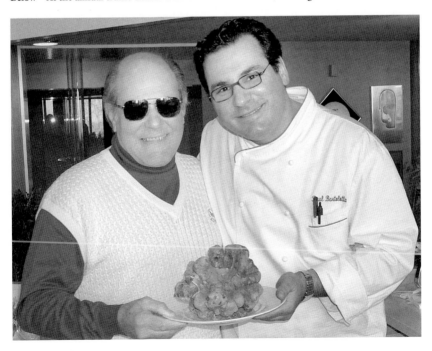

Above—From left, Michael Jordan, Tiger Woods, and Bill golfing at Olympia Fields Country Club in suburban Chicago.

Below—My son John and Ramsey Lewis preparing a lunch to celebrate my birthday.

Above—Enjoying dinner and the chef's company at Charlie Trotter's restaurant with Robert Mondavi.

Below—Tangley Oaks, Terlato Wines International Corporate Headquarters, Lake Bluff, Illinois.

Above—Preparing dinner at our Napa Valley home with (from left) Angelo Gaja and Bill.

Below—Inspecting new vines at Chimney Rock Winery with Doug Fletcher.

Above—2003: JoJo stands to my left as we prepare the Duck and Risotto Dinner in our Napa Valley home surrounded by our friends, from left: Gil Nichols, Robert and Margrit Mondavi, Garen Staglin, Nancy Andrus, Agustin Huneeus, Delia Viader, Naoko Dalla Valle, Dan Duckhorn, John Williams, Shari Staglin, Beth Nichols, Barbara Shafer, and John Shafer.

Below—2004: From left, Bill, Michel Chapoutier, and John join me in toasting the success of our joint venture with Chapoutier.

Above—2004: It was a pleasure to share the excitement of receiving the *Wine Spectator* Distinguished Service Award with some of my closest colleagues (from left): my assistant Carolyn Turnmire, John Kournetas, my son John, and John Scribner.

Below—2006: Surrounded by my wonderful family at the Horatio Alger award ceremony in Washington, D.C.

Our Corvo and Gancia distributor in New York was Peerless Distributing. Peerless was a family business run by John Magliocco and his brother Nino. Their father Tony had started the distributorship. During my appointment with John to present the wine, I told him we were preparing a Santa Margherita TV commercial for the Johnny Carson show.

"Carson's hot," he said.

"John, I'm looking for a 32,000 case order," I told him.

"You want 32,000 over twelve months?" he asked with disbelief.

"It is going to happen, John. Don't turn me down."

He considered my offer for a moment, and then told me he'd take 16,000 cases for the first six months. If I agreed to not force him to take the other 16,000 unless the first quantity had sold, we had a deal. I thought about it for a few minutes, and then we shook hands and went to dinner.

Of course, I was taking a tremendous risk. I was placing an order with Santa Margherita for 32,000 cases. If Magliocco didn't take the other 16,000 cases, I was stuck with them.

As I'd promised, we launched the TV commercial on *The Tonight Show* in 1981. The commercial showed me tasting Pinot Grigios in the Portogruaro restaurant where I'd first encountered the wine, saying, "I tasted eighteen Pinot Grigios and chose Santa Margherita as the absolute best." Within a few weeks, we ran magazine ads that supported the TV commercial.

We paid a lot of attention to the wine's image. We sold it as it deserved to be sold—as a luxury wine, with the bottle wrapped in silk. Another one of the ads pictured fresh coffee beans, pepper, and orange slices surrounding a bottle of Santa Margherita Pinot Grigio. The caption read, "If you like fresh ground coffee, fresh cracked pepper, or fresh orange juice, you will love Santa

Margherita Pinot Grigio." A radio campaign featured the first notes of Haydn's trumpet concerto played off-key, followed by an orchestra playing it beautifully. The announcer intoned, "If you could tell the difference between these two, you could tell the difference between Santa Margherita Pinot Grigio and all other white wines." Inspired by Chanel's ads, another ad asked, "Would there be a little black dress without Chanel? Would there be a Pinot Grigio without Santa Margherita?" Unfortunately, Chanel didn't care for the free advertising, so we continued the black dress ad—without mentioning Chanel.

Peerless placed Santa Margherita into every important Italian restaurant in the city, and after five months, Magliocco ordered the additional 16,000 cases. Seeing an opening, I asked him for a 40,000-case order for the next year. He answered me with his usual smile, but when I didn't return it, he knew I was serious. Peerless was already moving 30,000 cases of Corvo a year for me.

Magliocco grinned. "Okay. You have the order. Make sure you have a plan to expand the television ads."

We marketed it. We presented it. We helped package it. We made restaurateurs feel good about putting it on their wine lists and suggesting it to upscale customers. We made people feel good about drinking it and sharing it with friends—and we made sure everyone knew it was expensive. Even though the wine was priced at only $12 when we began representing it, it was three times more expensive than Italian white wine leaders Soave and Verdicchio, which at the time were selling for $3.98.

At a time when California Chardonnays were becoming bigger and more oaky, Pinot Grigio was a counterbalance. It is delicious to drink alone and pairs well with a variety of foods—grilled fish, scallops, clams, shrimp, chicken, or a simple dish of pasta. It has a little bit of citrus, a little bit of orange blossom, and a little bit of cantaloupe—flavor profiles people enjoy.

Pinot Grigio developed a life of its own. Everywhere I would go, when the conversation would turn to wine, someone would say, "I just discovered a wine that I'm absolutely in love with— Santa Margherita Pinot Grigio." Soon, Santa Margherita and Pinot Grigio became synonymous. Restaurant patrons would ask, "I'd like a bottle of Pinot Grigio." If the waiter brought a bottle that wasn't Santa Margherita, they'd reject it, saying, "The one I drink has a cream-colored label with a house on it."

Some might say that this market sensation "just happened," but today more than 110,000 wine labels are sold in the U.S. market. To stand out, you have to *make* it happen. Our first release was the 1979 vintage; by the time of the 1984 vintage's release, Santa Margherita Pinot Grigio was on everyone's lips. In *Wine Advocate*, Robert Parker wrote, "The white wines of Santa Margherita are the most striking examples I have tasted of the new breed of Italian whites...perhaps their greatest attribute is the one that is impossible to articulate properly—you just want to keep drinking them. If you want a quality benchmark for Italian white wines, these are your reference point."

Early on, we would occasionally lose restaurants who wanted to offer cheaper Pinot Grigios. Within a few weeks, most would call us back, saying, "The customers insisted on Santa Margherita, so it's back on the wine list." For many people, Santa Margherita Pinot Grigio is their favorite white wine, and why not? The wine is consistently good and continues to be one of the best values in white wine. It isn't often that you can buy the best wine in its category for less than $30 at a retail store.

Since 1979, farmers have planted hundreds of acres of Pinot Grigio and contracted to sell the grapes to Santa Margherita, which buys most of its grapes from the Alto Adige. The winemaker at Santa Margherita assembles different lots together with a plan to make a consistent taste profile year after year. The wine doesn't have a lot of aging, and the winemaker doesn't do much in the way of manipulation. I often think that if the company had anticipated how big Pinot Grigio would be, it probably would have purchased more of its own land. Today, Santa Margherita must pay premium prices for the best grapes. For the Pinot Grigio farmers, the wine's popularity has been tantamount to winning the lottery.

Our success with the Santa Margherita brand signaled our second transition up the industry ladder, from wholesaler to importer. Perhaps more importantly, the wine's success continued to identify our company with quality and gave us more national recognition. By 1984, Gancia, Corvo, Sicilian Gold, and Santa Margherita had firmly established Paterno Imports as an important U.S. importer of quality Italian wines.

Our growing national reputation became even clearer to me when I received a phone call from Mel Dick, who introduced himself as a distributor in Florida. Dick was interested in representing Paterno's brands throughout Florida and asked if he could come to Chicago and make a presentation. The usual practice was the other way around: We'd visit distributors and present *to them*. This was the first time a distributor had called us to ask for our brands. We set a date to meet in the near future.

When Dick visited our offices, it didn't take long for me to see that we were on the same page. Dick made a very impressive presentation, but I didn't want to appear too anxious. I told him I would have to think about it, and a few days later I called Dick to ask if I could see his operation. After all, Florida was a hot place, and fine wines don't like hot warehouses.

When I visited his operation, I found it to be quite impressive. We visited a few of Dick's accounts together, and as I had expected, he was well received by the trade. A month later, Southern Wine and Spirits became our Florida distributor. Today, Southern is a nationwide powerhouse and the largest wine and spirits distributor in the country. Dick is now the president of the company's wine division. Mel Dick remains a good friend of mine to this day, and his friendship now extends to my sons as well.

Success has its price, of course. I was now traveling to Italy at least three times a year and staying sometimes for more than a month at a time. This meant JoJo was often a single parent. She was the boys' authority figure, confidante, and a source of strength. Her work paid off—big time—but I sacrificed a lot of quality time with my sons.

I had committed to my father-in-law that I would move the business ahead and make it successful, but soon I discovered that not all of the Paterno family members were on the same page in terms of work ethic.

If a person wanted a conventional nine-to-five job that permitted him to go home, have dinner, and play with the kids every single night, the wine marketing/import business would invariably let him down. I worked hard and missed spending prime time with my wife and sons, and I expected the same from my partners, whether or not they were family members. (Perhaps they were not as passionate or committed to the business as I was.) I made an offer to the remaining Paterno family members who were still in the business: I would sell them my shares or buy out theirs. In the end, they chose to sell. At that point forward, I was on my own, with few financial resources immediately following the buyout. I quickly learned that in order for the business to grow, I'd have to invest every dollar of profit back into it.

SAUTÉED CLAMS

We like to pair this simple and delicious appetizer with Santa Margherita Pinot Grigio because the clean, crisp mineral flavors of the wine are very satisfying with the fresh-from-the-ocean clams.

SERVES A GROUP OF 8–12

24 little neck or Manila clams, cleaned

3 tablespoons olive oil

3 cloves garlic, sliced

1 teaspoon red pepper flakes

2 ounces water

2 ounces Terlato Family Vineyards Pinot Grigio

3 tablespoons parsley, chopped

Salt and pepper, to taste

Bread, crispy (as accompaniment)

1. Heat olive oil in a stock pot. Add red pepper flakes, salt, pepper, and garlic. Lightly brown garlic, add clams, stir, and keep covered for 2 minutes.

2. Add water, Pinot Grigio, and chopped parsley flakes and stir. Cover for 1 minute. Serve with crispy bread for dipping.

VARIATION

1. Cook some linguine *al dente* and pour this mixture over it for a first course.

SUGGESTED WINES

Santa Margherita Pinot Grigio, Terlato Family Vineyards Pinot Grigio, Boutari Moschofilero, Baglio di Pianetto Piana del Ginolfo

Toasted Ravioli

These fried, meat-filled pasta pillows served with a marinara sauce became a St. Louis original and staple, much like the ice cream cone. Although many claim to have invented this St. Louis treasure, Charlie Gitto declares, "Let there be no doubt, this baby is credited to Charlie Gitto's On The Hill."

As a mistake-turned-clever-invention, a cook dropped some cooked ravioli in bread crumbs by accident. Rather than toss it out, he deep-fried it to a golden brown color. At Charlie Gitto's, they still make the original recipe, but this version is a little easier.

Serves 4

1 cup milk

1 large egg, lightly beaten

2 cups dry Italian-seasoned bread crumbs

1 package meat ravioli

2 quarts vegetable oil for frying

Grated Parmigiano-Reggiano cheese

Fresh tomato sauce

1. Combine milk and egg in a bowl, making an egg wash. Place bread crumbs in a separate bowl. Dip frozen ravioli in milk wash and coat with bread crumbs.

2. Place in hot oil (350°F). Fry ravioli until golden brown.

3. Place on drainboard, sprinkle with Parmigiano-Reggiano cheese, and serve immediately with tomato sauce.

Suggested Wine

Santa Margherita Pinot Grigio

Casa Paterno, or Tony's Trattoria

A S THE 1980s PROGRESSED, PATERNO IMPORTS AND the Pacific Wine Company had acquired a terrific selection of important wines and improved their reach into French, Spanish, and German imports. In California, we were committed to Robert Mondavi, Charles Krug, and Beaulieu Vineyards. These commitments required a tremendous amount of infrastructure.

We stored thousands of fine wines in Pacific Wine's temperature-controlled cold room and 125,000-square-foot warehouse. We installed a sophisticated computer system to monitor all of our orders and transactions, and fully staffed departments handled public relations, art and design, legal, finance, sales, and marketing. By 1983, our sales staff increased from four divisions to nine.

Despite all this positive growth, I felt something was missing. In Europe, I had had the joy of experiencing the wonderful hospitality of Italian and French winemakers. They'd take me on tours of their wineries, taste their wines with me, and dine with me in the winery's dining room or the owner's home. It struck me as a great way to communicate with people.

Also, I firmly believed wine belonged with food, and I wanted our customers to be able to taste our wines with food in a dining room. I wanted to lose the informality and sterility of tasting them in an office behind a desk, and taking customers to restaurants didn't always work. I never had control over the situation. There were too many distractions. The waitstaff would inevitably interrupt at the wrong time, the chef might change the menu at the last minute, or the food would fight the wine I wanted to show off.

I also needed a relaxed place for staff to be able to taste, talk, and learn together over meals that showcased our wines—a place that was civilized and gracious and that could approximate the hospitality I had experienced with many of my European hosts.

Since the late 1960s, we had set up many tastings in our offices, with the wines accompanied by plates of prosciutto, cheese, and bread. After a while, I began experimenting with simple dishes: grilling steaks, boiling pasta, and making my grandmother's tomato sauce. (It's a wonderfully simple recipe: fresh tomatoes, chopped garlic, basil, parsley, and some olive oil cooked together for twelve minutes and seasoned with salt and pepper.) Cooking started to become a part of my workday, but it became a passion as well.

Eventually, I installed a small kitchen with a stove and grill on the second floor at Pacific Wine Company. It was a narrow room, but we had enough counter space for the prep work and plenty of pots and pans hanging from the ceiling. We transformed the computer room into a dining room, installing a beamed ceiling and a linoleum floor that looked like stone. The walls were refinished in rough stucco, and a chair-rail shelf displayed plates from famous restaurants around the world. On one wall stood a sideboard, and another wall featured a twenty-foot-long, floor-to-ceiling wine rack. Flanking the rack on both sides were two vintage wine-cask tops, gifts from Bob Mondavi.

In the center of the room, we installed a rustic hammered iron chandelier. The hand-hewn wood table underneath accommodated fifteen to twenty-five people. In time, we added a lounge with comfortable chairs and couches as a kind of foyer to the dining room—perfect for aperitifs and postprandial cigars and brandy. There was always background music—Caruso, Gigli, DeStefano, Callas, or Galli-Curci—played very softly and never intrusive, just to set the mood for elegant dining and elegant wines.

Soon, I couldn't pass a bookstore without buying a cookbook. My interest in pairing wines with appropriate dishes increased as our portfolio expanded to include more and more wines from France and California. I was spending three hours a day in the kitchen cooking for key management, staff, and guests. I was hooked. I loved playing chef, but I had a business to run, so I advertised in the local church bulletin for a cook who could prepare meals for our guests every day.

Shortly after, I hired Angela d'Argento. Her last name translates into English as "silver," and without a doubt, she was a treasure. She was from Rome and didn't speak much English, but she was round and adorable—a cute face, a terrific smile, and blonde hair. Everyone loved her, including JoJo. She had a magic touch in the kitchen, and she loved cooking. I had learned many recipes from my wife that she, in turn, had learned from my grandmother and her own mother, but still many of the Italian recipes that became part of my own personal cookbook came from d'Argento. We often worked together to create new recipes that were easy to prepare and matched our wines well.

She often tested me. "I'm going to make this tomato sauce with mushrooms. What shape pasta should I use?" I'd say orrechetti, and she'd say, "You're right." With another sauce, the right answer might have been fettuccine. She knew all the classic sauce-pasta pairings.

Sometimes I did have to remind her where the true focus should be. "Angela, too much salt, too much oregano, too much garlic. You have to cut it down." She'd argue that this was the way the dish should taste, but I'd counter, "Angela, you can't do that here. We are a wine company. Our goal is to show off the wine. You have to make dishes that work with the wine."

Little by little, she toned down the spices and garlic. She made a focaccia that was to die for, but it contained about a gallon of olive oil. She also used pounds and pounds of butter, but her sauces were always outstanding. Her salads sounded simple—tomatoes with Roquefort cheese, olive oil, and chopped purple onions, for example—but your mouth would water just thinking about them. Her bread was so crispy that it crunched, and she always served it with extra-virgin olive oil and freshly sliced tomatoes.

The many guests who visited our dining room didn't just have lunch—we were giving them a dining experience, and an unforgettable tasting experience. Often, we would line up as many as ten glasses in front of everyone at the table. "We're going to taste Italian, French, old vintage, new vintage, verticals of Château Lafite-Rothschild, and Renato Ratti Barolos."

Sometimes lunch lasted four or five hours, but they were working lunches. People were tasting our wine with the appropriate foods; we couldn't have devised a more effective kind of publicity. Occasionally, retailers would ask one another, "Have you ever been invited to lunch with Tony?" Anyone who said no would eventually let me know about it. "So, Tony, when am I going to be invited for lunch?"

I'd retort, "Well, how about next week?" Providing wine was never a problem, as Pacific Wine housed more than 200,000 cases from every wine-producing country in the world. Anything a guest wanted to taste, we would open.

Customers who were invited for lunch would occasionally stay until six o'clock in the evening. Sometimes we worried about how they were going to get home. So we decided to buy a car that would pick up customers—sometimes the manager of a store and two or three clerks, or a restaurant owner with his chef and maître d'—and stock it with Roederer Cristal on ice and crystal flutes. After lunch (and business), the chauffeur would drive them back to their business. As far as I know, we were the only importers and marketers in the country doing that at the time, and we did it at least twice a week.

Our way of doing business became the gold standard, especially with top local restaurants and Chicago retailers like Armanetti, Bragno World Wines, Foremost Liquors, Zimmerman's, and Party Mart. Of course, they often became my friends as well. We patronized their restaurants and stores and invited them back to taste new wines every year. Journalists were always welcome as well. We let them in on new arrivals, and we received excellent coverage in return.

———————————

On the days when we didn't have guests, the entire senior staff of the company—some eighteen people in all—would eat lunch together. It was a perfect opportunity to do blind tastings of three or four wines and discuss them. I never had a problem with our people drinking wine over a two-hour lunch, as these were intensely productive times that featured wide-open communication.

Over the years, the corporate dining room at Pacific Wine was the scene of many memorable meals. I remember well the day Lee Iacocca, then the chairman of the board of the Chrysler Corporation, visited. We thought the police officers stationed at every street corner around our building were there to protect him. (In reality, then-President Ronald Reagan was addressing a campaign rally nearby, and nearly every police detail in the city had been assigned to protect him.) During a brief meeting in my office, Iacocca talked about his vineyard, Villa Nicola in Brunello, and I learned about his passion for and understanding of wine and food. I was very impressed with his energy and love of food and wine. After comparing recipes, cooking together in the kitchen, reminiscing about Tuscany, and sharing wonderful wines, we enjoyed a wonderful lunch of *osso buco*. That day, we became the sole importer for Iacocca's Villa Nicola.

I also hosted many of the important wine producers who visited Chicago for trade events like the Italian Trade Commission's annual Il Vino competition. At Il Vino, our producers took home a lot of awards: Marchesi di Frescobaldi, the Mirafiore Tuscan wines, and our own Marsala took home medals. Il Poggione topped them all, taking home gold medals. To honor the prominent Italian and American wine producers who had assembled in Chicago to judge the competition, we prepared and served a wonderful dinner accompanied by a selection of fine French and California wines from my personal cellar, Cognacs, Armagnacs, and after-dinner cigars.

Other visitors to our dining room included food and wine writers Ruth Ellen Church and William Rice from the *Chicago Tribune*; Barbara Fairchild, the then-assistant editor and current editor-in-chief of *Bon Appétit;* and many chefs, including Charlie Trotter, Jovan Trboyevic from Jovan's, and Jean Joho from Everest, who taught me a lot about cooking and kitchens and remains one of my closest friends.

Over time, countless chefs from around the country also joined us in the kitchen. Every one of them had a secret. Joho once made a salmon dish that was so extraordinary, I told him I'd never tasted salmon that good before.

"When you're cooking salmon," he told me, "You have to put

it over the very lowest heat for about twenty minutes." In the past, I'd always seared the fish on both sides for ten minutes; now I follow his recipe and enjoy the results.

For years, I struggled with veal chops, which always turned out dry. When dining one evening in a restaurant in Palm Springs, a dining companion suggested that I order the veal chop. Reluctantly, I followed his advice, and the chop was indeed perfect. I asked the chef how he'd pulled it off, and his answer was surprisingly simple.

"I put it on the grill for less than a minute on each side, and in the meantime I pop a frying pan on the stove and bring it to a very high temperature with nothing in it. When the veal comes off the grill, I put it in the frying pan, shut off the heat, and put a cover on it. All the juices get trapped in the middle."

The fettuccine Alfredo served in most restaurants is usually pretty awful, but one restaurateur in New York served the best I'd ever had. I wondered aloud, "How can a chef make cream and butter taste so good?" After a few bottles of Champagne late one night, the restaurateur, Adi Giovanetti, told me his secret—he added a little veal stock to it.

For other preparations, such as making risotto, I used trial and error. Like it or not, properly prepared risotto takes eighteen minutes of standing and stirring. Broth is added three-quarters of a cup at a time, and there's more stirring and more broth added as the previous broth is absorbed. Rice releases its starch after twelve minutes, so from then on, other ingredients can be added, and the risotto cooks until it is creamy. Almost anything can be added to risotto—duck, mushrooms, chicken, shrimp, fennel. It was frequently a starting dish for us, and we found it to be a perfect companion to many of our white wines. For second courses, we'd serve either meat or game.

Over the years, we have served countless luminaries in the wine world, chefs, and restaurateurs at our headquarters. Many of them have graced our guest books with signatures, notes of gratitude, and, in a few cases, even drawings. Many of the food enthusiasts couldn't resist donning an apron and joining the fun in the kitchen. We entertained such luminaries as the Tuscan winemakers Marchese Leonardo Frescobaldi, Piero Antinori, and Baron Francesco Ricasoli; Count and Countess Alexandre de Lur-Saluces, owners of Château d'Yquem; Jean-Claude Vrinat, owner of the Paris restaurant Taillevent; Jean-Michel Cazes, legendary owner of the Bordeaux Grand Cru winery Château Lynch-Bages; and the Baroness Philippine de Rothschild. The baroness expressed her own inimitable style and exuberance in our guest book, writing, "Fascinating visit! Exhilarating wines! (Practically all Italian!) Unsurpassable pasta (finished it in the kitchen)! Incredible meat (bravo, Billy)! Super espresso … Thank you, Tony. When do I come back?" Christian Moueix, owner of Château Pétrus, and Bob Mondavi were also frequent guests throughout the 1970s and 1980s.

Count de Lur-Saluces and I were the same age, with birthdays only a few days apart. Dining with him and his wife, Berengere, was always noteworthy. On one occasion, I handed the countess an apron, and she surprised her husband by happily helping me make the sauce. The other guests on this occasion were Michael Broadbent, then the wine director at Christie's auction house in London, and his wife, Daphne. Our lunch began with prosciutto di Parma, accompanied by Roederer Champagne 1982. *Penne St. Martin* (see p. 199), a light pasta dish prepared with tomatoes, rosemary, mushrooms, and cream, set off a rich new white wine, Bianca di Valguarnera, from the producers of Corvo. A Heitz Cellars Cabernet Sauvignon Martha's Vineyard 1984 was perfectly supported by grilled beef tenderloin garnished with fresh crushed tomatoes, basil, and olive oil. For dessert, I chose a peach tart to partner with a Château d'Yquem 1983. (I searched for weeks before finding a suggestion by Andre Simon that peaches were perfect with young d'Yquem.)

At one particularly long lunch, Frank Schoonmaker was the guest of honor. Retailers Frank Armanetti and Eddie Bragno joined us, and after lunch we moved on to cigars and Cognac. Around six o'clock, Schoonmaker, Armanetti, and Bragno put their aprons on again and cooked dinner, which was followed by more cigars and Cognac. At midnight, Armanetti announced, "I'm hungry. Are there any leftovers?" We all ventured back into the kitchen again to make linguine, simply dressed with some olive oil, garlic, parsley, grated cheese, and ground pepper. It was a moveable feast—not in place, but in time.

A long lunch was the norm whenever Alexis Lichine was in town. On one occasion, we held blind tastings of some new vintage Burgundies from his superstar producers for a few hours. I started cooking the pasta while the group tallied the scores. Lichine, like most of us, loved pasta, so I'd made a rich Bolognese the night before his visit to make his meal memorable. After the pasta course, we grilled some double-ribbed lamb chops that paired beautifully with his Château Lascombes 1966—a touch he appreciated. We never finished a lunch with Lichine before dusk.

Bob Mondavi was also a frequent guest, and once in the early 1990s Chef Jean Joho and I prepared a dinner for Bob, his second wife, Margrit, and ten other guests to celebrate a first-place honor for his 1974 Cabernet Sauvignon. Our first course was a Florentine ravioli accompanied by a white 1934 Leroy Meursault Perrieres. The main course was a shell of beef, and I went all out with a 1947 Château Cheval Blanc. When he began to prepare the Chasseur sauce, Joho told me he'd need a bottle of whatever red wine I was going to serve at the dinner to add to the sauce.

I asked if we could make an exception that evening. "Who would know?"

"Only you and I," he said.

My heart broke as I watched the '47 Cheval Blanc go into the saucepan. When we served the sauce, I told my guests what they were about to consume. There wasn't a drop of sauce left on any plate. In the end, it was worth it, and Joho and I have been retelling the story ever since.

———————————

The dining room at Pacific Wine was not exactly a secret, but it *was* a secret weapon. My philosophy was, "Let's do something they will never forget." These lunches really allowed us to get to know our suppliers, buyers, restaurateurs, and distributors well, and vice versa. By extending our hospitality and our wines to them, we were able to forge a bond. What began as an experiment became an important part of my business philosophy. Exceptional wine and food pairings should bring to one's mouth what a symphony brings to one's ears. Such harmony occurs when a dish is properly paired with wine—all the herbs and flavors should blend until it is difficult to distinguish the dish's ingredients. If they're obvious, the chef has not created a true harmony.

The same is true with fine wine. There are certain elements that the winemaker wants to be identifiable. With age, a wine achieves a harmony of sensations and assumes its own unique bouquet and aromas, The taste of the particular varietal should be primary. The tannins of the wine and the flavors of the wood barrel it is aged in should be present, but subservient.

Wine pairings are subjective, and most people can do a fairly good job of it on their own. If three quality wines are considered for serving with a particular dish, usually one will pair better than the other two. That doesn't mean the other two aren't quality wines; it just means that one is better with that dish's particular flavors.

However, there are some elementary principles. Smoked salmon, which we frequently serve as a first course, doesn't pair well with overly fruity or herbal wines, so we serve it with oak-aged wines aged in heavily toasted barrels. As a result, they impart a slightly smoky character. There is a natural harmony between wines from a particular region and dishes made with vegetables and meat that are cultivated nearby. An olive-crusted leg of lamb pairs beautifully with a Rhône wine.

Of utmost importance to us was pairing the right dish with the wine we were profiling for our clients. Unlike most chefs and cookbook authors who prepare dishes and then selected wines to accompany them, we placed the importance on the wine and prepared the dish that would showcase it. I have to admit that in the 1960s and 1970s, I struggled with pairing California wines with California cuisine. The food looked beautiful on the plate, but because so much of it is based on vegetables, salads, and dressings, wine choices were difficult. There are certain ingredients that I personally find wine-unfriendly—cilantro, ginger, spinach, curry, and asparagus, for example—and I avoid them when we are showcasing a wine.

———

In addition to d'Argento, our sons Bill and John took turns at my side in the company kitchen. It was a wonderful experience to work with my sons in both the kitchen and the boardroom. Eventually, we hired a full-time professional chef, but I still always keep an apron handy.

My role in Pacific Wine's kitchen naturally spilled over into my home life as well. JoJo is an excellent cook, but on Saturdays I began to move into her kitchen to practice dishes, learn techniques, test sauces, and experiment with different cuts of meat. Soon, I was in the kitchen on Sundays as well.

Our refrigerator is always stocked with vegetables, tomatoes, and a selection of cheeses, including Roquefort, Parmigiano-Reggiano, and various goat cheeses. We always have prosciutto on hand, and fresh mushrooms because of their versatility (mushrooms make the perfect five-minute appetizer sautéed in butter with oregano, salt, pepper, red pepper flakes, and a few tablespoons of veal stock). We also keep many specialty items in our pantry—olive oils, mustards, balsamic vinegar, and perhaps thirty or forty different spices—so we're geared to cook and entertain at the drop of a hat.

Our freezer is stocked with lamb loins, lamb chops, New York strips, chopped round steak, and beef tenderloin. Alongside the meat, you'll find JoJo's famous pesto and veal, beef, and chicken stock. I'll often freeze some sauces of my own that take a particularly long time to prepare—lobster sauce, for example—and Colin Crowley, the Terlato corporate chef, often prepares sauces like Espanol, Chasseur, and green peppercorn sauce for my freezer at home.

My idea of the perfect fast lunch is a simple tomato salad with olive oil and a little bit of Roquefort cheese, fresh basil, diced purple onion, salt, and pepper with crusty bread. I have a great fondness for pasta and risotto dishes, too, because they can be made with a number of different ingredients. I can make a risotto with whatever's in the refrigerator—sometimes only cheese, mushrooms, and olive oil. Pasta is wonderful because it can be done so many different ways—one of my favorites is *Spirals alla Rustica* (see p. 216).

Of course, I don't ever think about a meal without first thinking about the wine. I frequently prepare lamb loins because they work so well with many wines. I bread them, sear them, serve a light mushroom sauce on top, or simply grill them with tomatoes, olive oil, basil, and a little bit of garlic.

In the late 1980s, a friend gave me a wok and an Asian cookbook. At first, I thought it was a strange gift, but one night, I said to JoJo, "Why don't we pick a recipe out of this cookbook and prepare it?" We made chicken breasts stir fried with vegetables, and it was the beginning of our love affair with Asian cooking. I was impressed by the dish's simple, healthy ingredients; it contained only a tablespoon of vegetable oil, some chicken stock, some soy sauce, and sesame oil.

Since I'm now a seasoned veteran of Asian cooking, I've got some favorites. I love to cook broccoli, celery, onions, sweet red peppers, snap peas, and grape tomatoes in the wok because all the greens stay green and the reds stay red, and everything remains crispy and flavorful. Another great plus of wok cooking is that it gets both of us in the kitchen doing the prep work. I'll open a half-bottle of champagne as we start to cut and chop, and JoJo will make the steamed rice. Once everything's cooked, we sprinkle some sesame oil on the finished vegetables and pour some more champagne. Sometimes, we'll add some fresh seared tuna with a little bit of garlic, soy sauce, and wasabi.

Christmas Eve is a favorite day in the kitchen, year in and year out. It always brought the entire family to our home—my parents, my in-laws, and JoJo's sister and children—for a family feast. I've cooked the same menu for the past forty-five years.

We feast on fish, clams, oysters, and a very special smoked salmon from the Outer Hebrides. Next, we dine on linguine with lobster sauce, which I first fell in love with more than forty-five years ago at a small Italian restaurant in Boston. The sauce was so good that I refused to leave without the recipe. It takes about five hours to make it, so I prepare it the night before (it's a favorite activity for our grandchildren). It cools overnight, and by the next day, the tomato sauce has absorbed all the flavor of the lobster—an unforgettable taste. Before reheating the sauce, I add some brandy, a little Sherry, chopped parsley, some red pepper, and olive oil. Every year, the grandchildren say, "Nonno, this is the best we've ever made."

Cooking has served me well in both my personal and professional life. In my opinion, nothing quite compares to a multigenerational dinner, with everyone celebrating a feast together. There's also the tremendous pleasure of spending a relaxed evening in the kitchen preparing a meal with JoJo. In terms of my business, our company's dining room has been a great boon—allowing us to share wonderful wines with delicious, well-matched foods with our business associates and friends. Many of my most treasured friendships have developed in the spirit of food and wine.

LINGUINE WITH LOBSTER SAUCE*

Traditionally, Italian families celebrate Christmas Eve with seafood. In our family, linguine with lobster sauce has always been the prelude to the festivities of Christmas. Even now, when our sons and their families join us in our kitchen, we always usher in the holidays by cooking linguine with lobster sauce.

SERVES 6

6 1-pound Maine lobsters, live

¼ cup extra-virgin olive oil

1 tablespoon butter

1 garlic clove, crushed

2 shallots, chopped

1 stalk celery, chopped

3 cans (28-ounce) Italian plum tomatoes, passed through food mill**

¾ tablespoon salt

¼ teaspoon tarragon

½ teaspoon red pepper flakes

1 cup white wine

3 ounces tomato paste

2 ounces brandy

1 tablespoon parsley, chopped

1¼ pounds linguine

1. Plunge live lobsters head-first into very large pot of boiling water; cover immediately and cook 8 to 10 minutes until they turn red. Remove from pot and cool slightly. Remove meat from tail and claws, and with heavy knife, chop shell and set aside in bowl.

2. In a large saucepan, heat oil and butter over medium-high heat until butter is melted. Sauté garlic, shallots, and celery in oil for 2 to 3 minutes, or until soft. Add tomatoes, salt, tarragon, and red pepper. Reduce heat to medium; cook 15 minutes. Add white wine, tomato paste, and brandy. Reduce heat to low; simmer 15 minutes.

3. Add the cut-up lobster shell, along with any juices that have collected in the bowl, to the sauce. Increase heat to medium; cook 30 minutes. Turn off heat and allow sauce to stand for 5 minutes. Remove lobster shells and discard. Strain through a mesh strainer; set aside on a heated dish.

4. Add parsley to sauce; cook over low heat to desired consistency (thick enough to coat a spoon). Season to taste.

5. Cook linguine in salted water until *al dente*, about 6 to 8 minutes. Drain linguine and combine with the sauce, adding ½ of the lobster meat. Spoon onto a warm serving platter and top with some of the cracked claws and tail meat. Serve remaining claws and tail meat in separate dishes.

SUGGESTED WINES***

Gaja Rossj-Bass, Langlois-Château Crémant de Loire Brut Rosé

* This recipe can be doubled.

** Alternatively, tomatoes may be coarsely processed in a food processor.

*** The flavor of the lobster sauce is so delicate that it requires a soft wine that is not aged.

PART IV

[1982–2008]

California Revisited

THE GREATEST DANGER FOR MOST OF US IS NOT THAT OUR AIM IS TOO HIGH
AND WE MISS IT, BUT THAT IT IS TOO LOW AND WE REACH IT.

—*Michelangelo*

IN MANY WAYS, MY FOCUS HAS ALWAYS BEEN ON salesmanship, and I have always known how important it is to reinvent the motivational wheel. I have also always firmly believed that as long as the people who worked with me were not only happy but also competitive, we would be successful.

Over the years, I learned that it was a good idea to ask prospective employees about their goals. If they replied that they wanted to upgrade their cars or refurnish their recreation room, the interview was over. Those dreams are too small. Our company needed people who dreamed of moving to upscale suburbs of Chicago like Winnetka or Kenilworth, of flying their own planes and piloting their own yachts, and of sending their children to the very best schools. The bigger their dreams, the harder they will work to achieve them.

I also devised a number of incentives to motivate our sales force. During our earliest years, I rewarded waiters for each bottle of our wine that they sold to their customers. "Simply save the corks, and we'll pay you a bonus for every one of them." As the business grew, the rewards also grew more desirable. For one challenge, I mailed letters to the homes of each of our salesmen offering a new home appliance for besting sales goals, knowing that the salesman's wife would open the mail and add a little incentive for her husband to increase his sales efforts. We also experimented with prizes like cars and trips to Europe for top sales performers.

In 1981, before the bottled-water craze hit the U.S. market, I began importing a sparkling Italian water called Ferrarelle. Supposedly, it was from a spring Julius Caesar frequented. I believed that bottled water would eventually take off, so I bought a 1,200-case container. At that point in time, we had absolutely no luck getting it into the market. It bombed.

To close it out, we gave two cases away with every five-case purchase of Gancia Asti Spumante. One day, a customer called John Kournetas, our sales manager, to complain. "I want the five cases of Asti, but please, no more free water. I can't give it away."

We were just a little early. Just as we were giving away the last cases, Kournetas and I attended the 1983 Restaurant Show at Chicago's McCormick Place. In one of the first large booths we came to, I noticed an enormous display of bottled water. I stopped in my tracks and nudged Kournetas. "Let's stop at that booth."

He looked at me in utter disbelief. "Oh, no, Tony. Not water again."

But I still had a good feeling about bottled water. After talking for a while with the representative, I invited him to Pacific Wine for lunch. As it turned out, he was looking for a distributor in Chicago, and after our lunch together, Pacific was chosen as the Evian distributor for the Chicago area. By 1986, we were moving more than 100,000 cases a year. The Ferrarelle joke was on me, of course, and for years, it gave us a good laugh.

It has never bothered me to identify mistakes I have made. I consider every mistake to be a learning experience rather than an embarrassment. However, I do get annoyed when I make the same mistake twice, especially with people. Doing so means I'm not paying attention. Usually, I can sense sincerity or deception in a person's tone of voice, or by looking straight into his or her eyes. Sometimes it's nothing more than a simple inflection made when replying to a question, or the way they sit, or how they move their arms. This sixth sense has always served me well in business.

———————

By 1986, sales of Santa Margherita Pinot Grigio in restaurants and retail stores were exceeding our expectations, and our reputation as a major U.S. importer of Italian wines was secure. However, in late 1986, a troubling incident shook up the Italian wine market. Methanol had been detected in some inexpensive wines bottled in Italy, and the U.S. government halted imports of Italian wines to the United States unless samples were analyzed from each container that arrived in the States. To add insult to injury, the *Chicago Tribune* ran on its front page a photo of several shelves of Italian wine draped in white sheets in a Walgreens drugstore. At the time, ninety-five percent of our sales were of Italian wines. Clearly, this was a message to expand our portfolio beyond Italy.

My first choice was California. In many ways, the timing was perfect, because the Wine Industry Technical Symposium had just invited me to speak at a meeting in Napa Valley. I asked the moderator, journalist Ed Everett, why he would want an importer to speak to California wine producers.

Everett answered without skipping a beat. "I want them to hear how an importer took an unknown grape varietal [Pinot Grigio] from Italy and made it one of the most popular white wines in the country, while California is struggling to sell Chardonnay for $6.00 a bottle."

At the symposium, I decided to talk about what I considered to be the two key factors for success in the wine business—"quality and discipline." I offered three points to the assembled group. The first was, "You're selling your wine too cheaply. You need to make it better, and charge more for it." Second, I asked them, "What do you want people to say about your wines five years from now? Whatever that goal is, act now to make it happen." Because consumption of California wine had been at a standstill for more than five years, my third point was, "If you want to grow your business in the next five years, you're going to have to steal business from the guys sitting on either side of you."

I made a lot of friends on that trip, but more importantly, I rediscovered California wines. After the convention was over, Everett asked me to accompany him on a tour of half a dozen wineries. During our conversation, he also suggested that I should buy a winery in the Napa Valley. Everett was convinced it would grow in importance, but I told him to forget it—I was happy importing and marketing wines. As I look back on it, his words must have left an impression somewhere in my mind.

The trip also proved to be valuable in another way. I tasted the '84s and some '85s. I was surprised to find that the wines had good structure, varietal purity, a middle body, and a lingering finish. They were much different than the California wines of the late 1970s and early 1980s. As I pondered the surprising new wines of California, I remembered Bob Mondavi's words: "It's about time you paid attention to California." At the end of my visit, I thanked Everett for a very interesting trip and told him I might eventually set my sights on California.

In the post-Prohibition era, California was slow to overcome its reputation for cheap wines and industry overreach. Frank Schoonmaker lambasted the state of the American wine industry in many of his writings. He condemned its use of generic labels and fictitious names and advocated providing information about grape varietals and geographic locations right on the bottle—Sonoma Pinot Noir instead of California Burgundy, for example.

Since Schoonmaker's manifestos, a continuing effort to upgrade the reputation of American wines from jugs of Chablis to Robert Mondavi's Fumé Blanc had been going on. In the 1960s and 1970s, a visible shift in generational leadership from fathers to sons took place in the Napa and Sonoma valleys. When the sons took over, many of them approached winemaking from a more scientific perspective, relying on research from the University of California at Davis and investing in improving their winemaking techniques by engaging international consultants like André Tchelistcheff.

Bob Mondavi was the trailblazer, building his Mission-styled winery in 1966 and concentrating his efforts on building a quality image for Napa Valley wines. His efforts turned the heads of even the most dedicated French wine enthusiasts: They quickly became aware that something important was happening in California. Statistics proved the point. By 1973, there were sixty-two wineries in Napa and Sonoma; twenty-one were a year old or less.

Steven Spurrier's blind comparative tasting of six Californian and four French wines in Paris on May 24, 1976, was a defining moment that dramatically highlighted the coming of age of California's Napa Valley wines. But public resistance remained.

According to most influential wine writers who wrote books on wine or contributed columns to the *New York Times* or *Gourmet,* the wines that still generated the most attention on both coasts were French. During this period, wine newsletters quickly grew into widely read publications, such as Marvin Shanken's *Wine Spectator*, that dramatically influenced what people drank. The 1982 Bordeaux vintage opened the wine futures market and launched Robert Parker and his newsletter, *Wine Advocate*, onto the international stage. Sometime later, Adam Strum's *Wine Enthusiast*, Stephen Tanzer's *International Wine Cellar*, and *Wine & Spirits* joined the ranks of important wine publications.

During the Reagan years, the dollar was strong against European currencies, and Americans flocked to Europe. Tourists sought out dining experiences from three-star dining rooms to bistros and trattorias and savored the local foods and wines. Back home, the same enthusiasts wanted to duplicate their experiences when they dined out—which meant ordering French and Italian wines.

By the mid-1980s, however, there was a noticeable shift from French cuisine to "made in America." Julia Child refocused her menus from French to American for her *Dinner at Julia's* television series. She made meals with California artichokes, chanterelles, and Pacific salmon, and interviewed California wine legends like Bob Mondavi, Louis Martini, and Dick Graff about what California wines were appropriate with dishes like grilled shrimp, roast saddle of veal, and chicken breast.

Impressed by what I had experienced in Napa and Sonoma, I returned to the West Coast several times over the next few months and tasted my way through some twenty-five wineries—Shafer, Clos Du Val, Heitz, Dominus Estate, Chappellet, Hess Collection, Spottswoode, Jordan, Château St. Jean, Ferrari-Carano, Stags' Leap, Arrowood, Pine Ridge, Schramsberg, and a host of others. I encouraged each winery to join me at Pacific Wine Company, and they all did. I truly believe they could see my passion for quality wines, and now, after so many years of focusing that passion on the wines of Europe, I was redirecting it to California wines. These trips began a renewed love affair with the wines of California.

In Napa, Chardonnay and Cabernet Sauvignon were the grapes of choice. So my choice of a varietal in 1986 for us to market nationally was Pinot Noir, a grape that at that time was still under the radar. My sons and I invited John Scribner to join us in tasting all the Pinot Noirs that were available. We found one that impressed us all—Williams Selyem. I made an appointment with the winery, which was located in northern Sonoma County. When Scribner and I arrived at the address we'd been given, we couldn't find a winery. We entered the closest address, an architect's office, and asked if they knew where we could find the Williams Selyem winery. He replied, "You found it. It's in the garage out back."

Sure enough, Ed Selyem was waiting there for us. He was surrounded by salvaged dairy equipment and the secondhand stuff that the men had accumulated to make their "cult" wine. We tasted Pinot Noirs from a number of barrels, and they were all terrific, with a nice body, good mouthfeel, and wonderful aromas. I told Selyem that I wanted to be his agent for the United States, but he replied that we would have to come back the next week to meet his partner, Burt Williams, before he could make any decisions about distribution.

When I returned to California the next week, I brought along Bill. I had learned that Williams, a former pressman at the *San Francisco Chronicle*, liked Grappa, so we brought along a nice bottle from our collection as a gift. We talked for a while, and finally, Selyem said they could give us ten cases of Pinot Noir and fifteen cases of Zinfandel a year for the Chicago market.

Surprised, I explained that although I thought their offer was better than nothing, I was looking for a Pinot Noir to market for the entire country. Eventually, I said, "Pacific Wine will be happy to sell your Pinot Noir and Zinfandel in Chicago."

While we were talking, I noticed large letters written in chalk on the barrels: A on some, and R on others. I asked what the letters meant. Selyem replied that the "A" was for grapes they had purchased from Allen Vineyards, and the "R" was for Rochioli Vineyards, farmed by Joe Rochioli and his son Tom near the Russian

River. I remembered that Burt Kallick, the owner of Le Chiminée Restaurant in Chicago, had raved about Rochioli's wines.

As we drove away from the Williams Selyem winery, I called Kallick in Chicago. I told him where we were and asked him if he could arrange a meeting at Rochioli for us. Within a few minutes, he called back and said that Tom Rochioli was at the winery and waiting for us. We made a U-turn and headed for the Russian River Valley.

Bill and I hit it off right away with Rochioli, a down-to-earth guy. After tasting his Pinot Noir, with its black cherry aromas, pronounced spiciness, and rich soft velvety textures. At the time, Rochioli produced only 462 Pinot Noir cases a year, but he also had a larger amount of a wonderful, Sancerre-style Sauvignon Blanc and a fruity, lean, Burgundian-style Chardonnay. Rochioli wanted to make the wine without being involved in the business of selling it. We were in business to market and sell wine without the headaches of making it. We quickly realized that it was a match made in heaven.

Bill, John Scribner, and I returned to the Rochiolis' vineyard the following week with a prepared agreement, and we invited Tom Rochioli, his father Joe, and their wives to dinner at a nearby restaurant. During the course of the meal, we made some minor handwritten changes in the agreement. Scribner said, "I'll rewrite the agreement and mail two sets signed by us for you to sign. Keep one copy, and mail the other one back to us."

More than eager to execute the deal, I asked, "What's the difference if there are lines and arrows? Let's sign them right now." But Scribner was a stickler for professional protocol and wanted to rewrite the contract, and I understood.

When I arrived at my office on Monday morning, I found the new *Wine Spectator* on my desk. I glanced at the front cover and read the headline: "California's Best Pinot Noirs." There were three bottles on the cover—Calera, Saintsbury, and the 1985 Rochioli Pinot Noir.

Rochioli didn't need a marketing agent for his 462 cases a year. I asked Scribner if the agreement had been sent. He answered that it had, by registered mail. On Wednesday, I called Rochioli. "I don't think you need us anymore," I told him. "If you don't sign the document, I'll understand."

Without hesitating, he said, "Sure, I can sell every case today just to fill the phone calls I'm getting, but I'm going to be around for a long time. We made a deal. I make the wine; you sell it. I want you to keep your commitment."

The quality of Rochioli's wines was exceeded only by the quality of his ethics. Rochioli's production was limited, but the wines were outstanding—it was exactly the kind of partnership we wanted.

We would continue to revisit the California wine scene over and over again, but along the way, we got sidetracked by a young French winemaker who matched Tom Rochioli's serious winemaking skills and dedication to quality.

———————

Although high in quality, our recent California acquisitions came in limited quantities, so I decided to return to France in 1987 to explore areas beyond Bordeaux and Burgundy. Knowing where I was headed, a friend mentioned that the venerable Rhône Valley winery Domaine Chapoutier was considering changing its U.S. agent. I remembered Chapoutier's Châteauneuf-du-Pape La Bernadine, a marvelous wine that had sold well in my father's store in the late 1950s. Chapoutier wasn't very far from Tain-l'Hermitage, one of my destinations, so my friend made an appointment for me to visit.

I toured the winery and cellars with the senior Chapoutier, Max. Chapoutier cultivated the five hundred acres of vineyards the family had accumulated over the past two hundred years and also acted as a *négociant*, a man who uses the grapes or bulk wine of other farmers to make his own wine. As we talked, it became clear to me that sales were slow—I could feel the lack of vigor.

Before going to dinner at his home, Max took me to the laboratory to meet his son Michel. Michel, twenty-five years old, was the younger of Max's two sons. He was a five-foot-six bundle of energy who had graduated from oenology school in France and had served internships at various California wineries. He was also a farm boy who was wise well beyond his years. We began talking, and before I knew it, it was after nine and we still hadn't gone to dinner.

Over dinner, young Chapoutier mesmerized me with his ideas about biodynamic farming—letting the site and soil speak for itself. He wanted to ban the use of sprays and chemicals in winemaking and apply homeopathic ideas to the science of creating wine. After dinner, we talked until midnight.

I called my son Bill the next morning, telling him, "I met a genius last night. Not the father, but the son. The Chapoutiers are down to about 600 cases a year in sales in the States. I'm sure this winery can become one of the top-quality brands again. When Michel bottles his 1987 harvest, the results will be outstanding."

Michel Chapoutier was an honest young man, and when we spoke the next day, he told me that upon graduating from oenology school, he'd returned to find that the winery was having some financial difficulties. If I took the brand, Chapoutier said, it would be necessary to pay in advance for the container of wine in order to satisfy his bank.

When I returned home, I told our bank I'd be paying in advance. A few days later, I got a call from one of the bank's officers, who questioned the wisdom of paying in advance for a wine that had not yet been shipped from a company with deep financial problems. To make matters worse, I had contracted for more cases than the winery had sold in total for the preceding two years, and I was buying the 600 cases that remained in the current importer's inventory. I guess he was right to question what was going on.

I replied, "I'm betting that this young man is going to make great wines one day, and that he won't forget what I did for him."

The first vintage we bought was 1985. It was very ordinary, as was the 1986. When Chapoutier came to the States in early 1989 to do a tasting tour, my sales manager called from California to tell me Chapoutier planned to taste only the 1988 vintage. It was the first year he had totally controlled the production, and he wanted the wine world to see what he was doing. He refused to taste the 1985 vintage with the trade.

This was a huge problem for us, because we were loaded with 1985 and 1986. When Chapoutier arrived in Chicago, I asked him to explain. He said, "Tony, the '85 and '86 were not my wines. They were made by my father. I can't tell the trade that they are good, because they're not. I can't say they are not good, because it would embarrass my father."

Of course, I was in a bind. He was being honest with me and protecting his father. We did the right thing and reduced the prices on both '85 and '86 vintages to close them out.

The younger Chapoutier's first vintage year, 1988, was ordinary for the rest of the Rhône Valley, but the wine he made was outstanding. I remembered a wise quote from the wine journalist Robert Parker: "You can tell the great winemakers by how good their wines are in poor vintage years." Michel Chapoutier proved the point.

Two years later, Christine King, then the head of our public relations department, persuaded Robert Parker to visit Chapoutier on his Rhône tasting tour. He told her he was too busy for a tasting, but he would stop by to say hello for fifteen minutes. Legend has it that he stayed for eleven hours, and shortly after his visit, he wrote that Michel Chapoutier was one of the "best winemakers on the planet." Shortly after the article appeared, Chapoutier's single-vineyard estate wines became the most sought-after wines of the Hermitage appellation.

By the end of the 1980s, our sales force numbered 120. We had turned our attention to California; we now represented Rochioli and had acquired Chapoutier from France, but I realized we also needed to include selections from the world's other wine-growing regions. At Kournetas's suggestion, we tasted numerous wines from Greece and added the wines of Boutari to our portfolio. In particular, I believed their white wine Moschofilero had the potential to change the way the market viewed the wines of Greece. Toward the end of the decade, we bought another Illinois distributor, Mid-Continent, and changed its name to Vintage Wine. This acquisition added the brands Duckhorn, Silver Oak, Iron Horse, Frog's Leap, and a number of other outstanding California vineyards to our portfolio.

In ten short years, we had dramatically increased our presence on Chicago's restaurant wine lists. We had well-chosen imports and had expanded our distributorships. Most importantly, I had rediscovered California wine and met Michel Chapoutier. Both would play important roles in our future.

PENNE ST. MARTIN

I first tasted this dish on the island of St. Martin, and it became so much a part of my cooking repertoire that I made it to celebrate a luncheon visit with the Count and Countess Alexandre de Lur-Saluces (see p. 176).

SERVES 6–8 AS A FIRST COURSE

½ cup olive oil

1 tablespoon butter

3 cloves garlic, cut in half

Salt and pepper, to taste

6 ounces brown button mushrooms, quartered

1 can (32-ounce) plum tomatoes, cored and drained

1 cup shelled peas

1 sprig fresh rosemary, leaves removed and minced

5–6 fresh basil leaves, finely chopped

Pinch of red pepper

1 pound penne pasta, dried

⅓ cup heavy cream

¾ cup freshly grated Parmigiano-Reggiano cheese

1. In a saucepan, heat the olive oil and butter with the garlic and a pinch of salt and pepper. When the garlic is lightly browned, remove the pieces and discard.

2. Add mushrooms and cook until they release their liquid.

3. Add the tomatoes and simmer for 10 minutes, or until soft.

4. Bring water to boil in a large pot.

5. Add the peas, rosemary, basil, red pepper, salt, and pepper, and cook an additional 5 minutes, or until peas are tender.

6. Add salt and penne to boiling water while sauce is cooking. Cook pasta until tender or *al dente*. Drain and transfer to a serving bowl.

7. While pasta is cooking, add cream to the sauce, stir, and cook until heated through.

8. Pour hot sauce over penne, add half of the Parmigiano-Reggiano cheese, and toss. Garnish with remaining Parmigiano-Reggiano cheese.

SUGGESTED WINES

Il Poggione Rosso di Montalcino, Tamarí Malbec, Chimney Rock Cabernet Sauvignon.

Father and Sons

LIVE SO THAT WHEN YOUR CHILDREN THINK OF FAIRNESS, LOVE, CARING,
AND INTEGRITY, THEY THINK OF YOU.

—H. Jackson Brown, Jr.

U NFORTUNATELY, "BLOOD-AND-WINE" STORIES OF
Napa and Sonoma family feuds are commonplace.
Because of them, a part of me was always apprehensive
about one or both of our sons joining me in the wine business. I
set that aside when I found out that our older son, Bill, wanted
to work with me at Pacific Wine after graduating from Loyola
University in December 1981. I was overjoyed about the idea of
driving to work with him in the morning—and banking on the
fact that the principles I had always taught him to follow would
prevent us from having serious disagreements.

The importance of selecting a profession and working hard to
get a law or medical degree was something I'd always talked to
my boys about. I suppose it went back to my father's desire to
be a lawyer, and his disappointment about having to leave law
school during the Depression. Perhaps it was also a response to my
own indifference about college. I never encouraged my sons to join
the company—I only wanted them to study, get a degree, and do
whatever was necessary to have a good career and create success for
themselves and their families.

During his last two years at Loyola, Bill scheduled his classes for
the morning hours, leaving the afternoons open to attend classes

of a different kind at Pacific Wine. My own father was also retired, but he came to the offices of Pacific Wine every day. My father, Bill, and I would have lunch together daily with the management team. Bill got to know all of the employees and enjoyed the time he spent with his grandfather and me. Bill's understanding of computers came in quite handy. Since computers were increasingly becoming essential to virtually every aspect of our business, he began to develop a formalized reporting system timeline that gave us the capability to track customer sales, orders, and inventory on a daily basis.

After graduation, Bill planned to go on to law school, but since he graduated from college during the winter, he decided to wait to begin school until the regular term began in September. We both figured that working as a salesman for Pacific Wine would be good experience in the meantime.

Many of my friends and employees thought I would give him the most prized territory in the company, but instead, I gave him the worst one, with the longest commute. My move surprised everyone, including Bill. I told him he shouldn't have to carry the burden knowing the other employees would think, "Sure, the son gets preferential treatment." It would be far better for them to ask, "Why do you treat him so badly?"

Bill understood and said, "Don't worry, Dad, I'll make it one of the best territories in the company." He did, even though working in Lake and McHenry counties meant trying to convince bowling alleys, truck stops, small retail stores, and taverns to buy fine wines from Italy and France. He loved the challenge, so much so that sometime between January and August, Bill knew he wasn't going to go to law school, after all—he wanted to be a part of the business permanently. It was a tough conversation, but he told me that after the first two weeks at Pacific, he knew selling and being with people was what he wanted to do. At the time, John had one more year to go at Loyola University. Afterward, he planned to go to Arizona State to study architecture.

Since New York was our most important market, Paterno Imports had an office in the Time-Life Building on Sixth Avenue, so after Bill had spent about nine months at Pacific Wine, I thought he would benefit by jumping into a big pond with the big fish. Santa Margherita sales were just picking up in the New York market. I thought it was time for Bill to put his sales training at Pacific Wine to use at Paterno Imports. For the next six months, he'd be monitoring how successful the distributors were with moving their inventory—a pretty complicated task. In this way, he'd learn firsthand about how important distributors really are.

I also remembered something my good friend Jackson Smart had told me many years before. "Get your sons away from you for a while, so they can find out how other people visualize your work and perceive the company." When Bill asked if he could spend some time in New York, I agreed and offered him the position of Santa Margherita's brand manager. Without hesitation, he accepted.

Of course, Bill's move to New York was a painful time for JoJo, John, and me. We were a close family, and it was the first time any of us had been separated. I found a lot of good reasons to visit New York often. We spoke almost every day, and just hearing his voice warmed my heart.

In his new role, Bill initiated numerous programs that accelerated the growth of Santa Margherita. As the brand manager, he began to ask all the right questions: "What is the strategic vision for this brand?" "How can we implement programs over a calendar year and track them?"

Eventually, he came up with a really unusual idea for Santa

Margherita. At a time when everyone else was using transistor radios and similar prizes to motivate their salespeople, he came up with a program that offered different sizes of diamonds to our salespeople depending on their level of distribution and the quantity of their placements. JoJo used her connections in the jewelry business to get jewelers' bags for us, and we purchased a variety of diamonds from a diamond wholesaler. The diamonds were graded in terms of size and color and clarity, and of course, the best ones were more costly. We set up a display of the diamonds for the salespeople and showed how they could earn them.

First, Bill asked the sales team how many cases of Santa Margherita they planned to sell and how many placements they'd secure for the wine in restaurants. If a salesperson answered, "I'm going to sell a hundred and fifty cases and get sixty placements," Bill would reply, "That will entitle you to two one-carat diamonds."

Next, we laid out incentives for them to earn more expensive diamonds and made our pitch. "If you're willing to commit to the goal, we'll give you the diamonds right now. If you don't achieve it, you'll have to pay us for them or give them back."

Some of the salespeople were reluctant to sign those agreements, but others jumped at the chance. We knew that the salespeople who chose to sign would never have to pay for those diamonds, and that they would find a way to make their goal or be embarrassed in front of their wives. The results were incredible. Excitement about the brand was contagious, and the diamond sales incentive program created an image for the brand: Santa Margherita was associated with diamonds, and many competing brands were still associated with transistor radios and toasters.

Bill quickly moved up from brand manager to manager of our eastern division's sales force, and he was soon back in the Chicago office. After his return, he told me, "Distributors are busy with too many accounts. We need to beef up our sales with an extra layer of sales reps who don't call on the distributor and instead work directly on the trade. All they'll do is work the accounts—especially the largest ones—and firm up those relationships. Ultimately, we have to control the relationship with the account."

I realized that his strategy was an extension of our policy of making wine lists for restaurants and bringing prospective accounts and distributors to our company dining room to present our wines in the best possible way. His idea was a good one, so we expanded the sales force around the country and created a role for district managers who called on accounts directly.

During his time in New York, Bill also spent a good bit of time thinking about the company's position in the market. "We're starting to build up a lot of brands," he said, "but no one should have a better Italian portfolio than we do." He believed that in order to corner the market on quality Italian wines, we should have the best brand from each viticultural area of Italy. That struck a chord with me, and so I aggressively pursued the high end of the Italian wine market in every viticultural area.

As I think back on it now, Bill was beginning to carve out an area for himself in the company. I knew things wouldn't always be easy for him, but I also knew he had to make a statement of his own. When the national sales manager tried to undercut Bill's authority, Bill came to me. I responded that it was his own responsibility to earn the respect of others. If I intervened, it would diminish his importance. To his credit, he agreed.

I promoted Bill to national sales manager in 1985, the year after he married Debbie Cerone, the daughter of longtime friends of ours. The difference in their ages was huge when they were nine and six years old, but by the time Bill was twenty-two and Debbie was nineteen, their age difference no longer mattered, and they started dating. They had the same values, both had been part of our close-knit Italian community in Chicago, and when they married, JoJo and I gained the daughter we'd never had. A year later, our first granddaughter was born and named JoJo, after her grandmother. I had the deep satisfaction of holding a grandchild in my arms for the first time.

The next generation had arrived, and we became professional grandparents. JoJo and I sold our condominium at Lake Geneva and bought a lovely home on the lake so our granddaughter and other future grandchildren would have a lawn to play on.

When Bill, Debbie, and little JoJo moved from their condominium in Lincolnwood to their new home in Lake Forest in 1987, my wife, JoJo, and I decided to move to Lake Forest as well. After all, our household had expanded, too. I had grown up in a multigenerational home and worked in a multigenerational business. I always liked the mix of old and young, and I can't imagine what it would have been like if my grandmother hadn't lived with us during my childhood. When my father passed away in 1983, my mother was lost. Someone she had been with day in and day out for 50 years was suddenly missing from her life, so JoJo and I invited her to live with us. My mother devoted herself to her grandsons and great-grandchildren, and the multigenerational tradition continued.

As the years went on, we were fortunate to become involved in many civic and charitable organizations in the city, like the wine auctions that supported the Lyric Opera of Chicago. We had been friendly with Chicago's longtime mayor, Richard J. Daley, during his administration, and we eventually got to know his son, the current Chicago mayor Richard M. Daley, and his family.

We were also invited to participate in events sponsored by various wine and food groups. I vividly remember the night Michael Broadbent, the legendary wine critic and author, served as the honorary auctioneer for the Lyric Opera. I took advantage of the opportunity to invite him to join us at our headquarters for a tasting and luncheon. I had met him many times before, but entertaining him in our corporate kitchen and tasting wines with him was a great experience.

On another occasion, we had the pleasure of entertaining Julia Child. She sat on the board of the American Institute of Wine and Food, and when the organization's Executive Committee met in Chicago in December 1988, both Child and Bob Mondavi accepted an invitation to lunch at our corporate headquarters at 2701 S. Western Avenue. Child signed our guest book with the words, "The best Christmas lunch of the season! Thanks for everything!!"

Our higher visibility and the growing appeal of wine and food societies like the American Institute of Wine and Food also led to one of our most enduring associations, which is still a continuing source of satisfaction for me. In 1995, a few years after the Italian restaurant Coco Pazzo opened in Chicago, I was asked to host a Confrérie des Chevaliers du Tastevin dinner there spotlighting Burgundy wines. I balked at first, knowing it is difficult to match French wines to an Italian menu, but the Confrérie's *Grand Sénéchal* (leader), Allan Bulley, cajoled me into choosing Burgundies from their cellar to accommodate an Italian menu. Against my better judgment, I agreed to chair the event. I met with the chef to talk about pairings and taste their wine and food. The wine was good, the food was absolutely wonderful, and the chef, a giant of a man, was brilliant. Resigned to our task, we tasted the wine and food together and struggled to make matches.

The night of the dinner, I apologized to the group. Both the wine and food were delicious, but they didn't pair well. I believe successful pairings involve wines and foods nurtured by the same soil and weather, and a synergy exists between them. If you prepare a French recipe, you drink a French wine. To me, the dinner had no synergy and just didn't work. I said, "I'm sorry. I shouldn't have done this. An Italian kitchen deserves to have Italian wines, and these French wines deserve a French kitchen."

At that moment, John Richman, who was at the time the chairman of Kraft Foods, said to me, "Why don't you create an Italian gastronomical society that showcases Italian wines and food? You form the group, and I'll be the first member." Ten other hands went up.

With that, the Renaissance Club was born. The group, which is limited to thirty members (thirty is the "magic number" that most chefs agree is the perfect size for an extraordinary meal), was founded with the mission of exploring foods and wines of various regions of Italy, such as Piedmont, Venezia, Sicily, and Tuscany. At its inaugural dinner, which was held at the Italian restaurant Spiaggia, each member was initiated by a tap on the shoulder with a sword, and members received Renaissance Club medallions. The meal was prepared by Spiaggia's chef, Paul Bartolotta, a man with a great command of the cuisines of the different regions in Italy.

I believe that when I go to a restaurant for dinner, it's the chef's kitchen. It's up to me to find a wine that pairs well with his food. At a Renaissance Club dinner, however, the wine is the tenor and the food is the chorus. The better chefs understand this subtlety perfectly. Before a dinner held at the Drake Hotel, Leo Waldemeier, the chef told me, "I love this. It's a challenge. When my staff hosts a dinner for the Renaissance Club, they're tested; they're pushed. They have to use their imaginations. I love it when they're able to break out of the mold."

The members of the Renaissance Club have high expectations and a strong appreciation that gastronomy is an art and wine is an essential part of the pleasure of dining. Members have raved for years about one particular Renaissance dinner at the Italian Village restaurant. The chef at the Italian Village totally understood the concept. At that dinner, I realized why the name we had given to the group was so appropriate. Renaissance means rebirth, and we were breathing new life into the centuries-old tradition of pairing regional dishes with well-matched wines of the same region.

I approached the notion of creating a wine cellar for the Renaissance Club with great excitement. I belong to the Commanderie de Bordeaux aux États-Unis, a confederation of Bordeaux wine aficionados, as well as the Confrérie des Chevaliers du Tastevin, a group of Burgundian enthusiasts. The Commanderie has a fantastic wine cellar made up of thirty-, forty-, and fifty-year-old Bordeaux wines that are still very much alive and still taste important. When I created the cellar for the Renaissance Club, I followed the Commanderie's model and put together the very best Italian producers and the very best vintages.

My old friend Renato Ratti told me years ago that you should taste a wine when it's twelve years old and then determine how much longer you want to keep it, because at twelve years, it's either going to get a lot better, or a lot worse. Today, the Renaissance cellar has wines that date back to the 1970s. We try to drink many of them when they have aged for twelve to fifteen years, with the exception of Brunellos, Barbarescos, and Barolos, which we age longer.

Besides enhancing members' appreciation of the gastronomic delights of Italy, the Renaissance Club offers other diversions. Chef Paul Bartolotta prepares a White Truffle Dinner to coincide with white-truffle season in Piedmont. White truffles cost several hundred dollars a pound, depending on the quality and quantity of the crop that year. The White Truffle Dinner costs around $500 a person, but the dinner is always the best-attended event of the year. Every year, the dinner reminds me of the truffles I'd shared with my father-in-law in Italy.

We also host an annual Renaissance Club pig roast on the grounds of Terlato Wines' headquarters. All the guests wear red, white, and/or black. The chef arrives at five in the morning to start roasting the pig, and by four in the afternoon, it's ready. We start the evening with a tasting of fifteen to twenty different wines from the Renaissance cellar. After the wine tasting begins, we play bocce on the lawn and enjoy live music, sometimes from a three-piece combo or an accordion player. One year, we even had an organ grinder, complete with monkey.

Today, the Renaissance Club hosts five black-tie dinners each year. The concept was to focus on Italian recipes prepared in fine restaurants—and not necessarily Italian ones. We provide the restaurants with the wines, the chef tastes them, and we leave it up to the chef to create the dishes that will pair best with the wines. One week before the dinner, the two chairs of the dinner, the owner of the restaurant, and I participate in a test lunch to discuss the success of the pairings.

A few of the restaurants we have selected over the years include Charlie Trotter's, Everest, Gabriel's, Gianotti's, the Ritz-Carlton, Spago, and the Four Seasons. Once, Lidia Bastianich of New York's Felidia and Piero Selvaggio of Valentino's in Los Angeles teamed up to prepare a dinner for the group in our corporate dining room. In February 2008, we celebrated our eighty-seventh *riunione* at the Four Seasons.

As we planned the menu for one of those eighty-seven dinners,

I asked the chef (who shall remain nameless) to prepare *osso buco*.

He replied, "That's very boring."

Somewhat surprised, I replied, "Well, why don't I take the boredom out of it? Why don't you make the best Ossobuco I've ever had in my life?"

It was his turn to be taken aback. He apologized and swore that he would make the best braised veal shin anybody had ever eaten—and I must say, he did.

As our business expanded, our family's involvement in it continued to grow as well. After graduating from college, John went on to attend John Marshall Law School, passed the bar, and took a position in the commercial real estate division of Sears. His interest was in real estate development because of its natural connection to his love of architecture.

After a while, he began to feel that the career didn't suit him. He decided to join Pacific Wine in 1989, and I was very pleased. He worked with the sales reps and focused considerable efforts on overhauling and modernizing the operations side of the Pacific Wine Company. More than ever before, I felt a responsibility to grow the company to provide for Bill's growing family and John's future one.

The 1990s became a decade of great expansion, as Paterno Imports evolved into a full-service marketing company and further expanded its portfolio. We gradually acquired four more wine distribution companies, thus providing coverage of the entire state of Illinois. These acquisitions helped strengthen an already strong restaurant presence in Illinois.

In 1991, I was invited to a friend's house to watch a football game. Everyone was drinking beer. I've never cared much for beer, because the taste just doesn't appeal to me. But I figured, when in Rome, do as the Romans do, so I grabbed a bottle and poured it into a glass. Much to my surprise, I liked it. I asked my host where he had gotten the beer, and he replied that he'd tried it on the East Coast and liked it so much, he'd ordered a few cases to be shipped to him in Chicago.

A few days later, I checked out the beer company. The founder of the company was a young lawyer named Jim Koch; I tracked down his number and gave him a call. I introduced myself, told him about our company, and asked if he had a distributor in Chicago. He replied that he did, and said that at that time, his distributor was selling 60,000 cases a year in Chicago. I felt that I could do better than that, and invited him to lunch the next time he was in Chicago.

Shortly thereafter, he joined me for lunch at our headquarters. I quickly learned that like me, his focus was on quality. We were a wine company, I told him, and we'd never sold beer before, but I knew we could sell this one.

He thought for a moment and then replied, "I believe you can, too." Within a few days, we had a signed agreement. The beer was Samuel Adams.

After we landed Samuel Adams, my son John followed in his brother's footsteps, becoming the brand manager for the beer. (Maybe it was a lawyer-to-lawyer connection.)

As part of his strategy, John challenged the wine team, saying, "Can you sell beer?" The answer was a resounding yes. By 1996, he had increased the sales from 60,000 cases to an astounding 800,000 cases of Samuel Adams beer a year, and Koch set a new goal for the following year of 1.5 million cases. If we reached Koch's goal, I realized that we would morph from a wine company selling beer to a beer company selling wine, and beer sales would overwhelm our fine wine business. I told Koch it was time for us to sell the Samuel Adams franchise to a beer distribution company. He realized our predicament and helped us move forward with the sale.

Bill and John worked together on the negotiation for the sale of the franchise and came up with an innovative deal. Instead of holding an auction, which would have been the normal procedure, they had the interested companies submit sealed bids, with no second offer accepted. Chris Reyes, the largest Miller distributor in the States, presented the highest bid. Other bidders subsequently countered with higher bids, but we kept our word.

After the sale, everyone was pleased with the outcome, including Koch. Bill and John have since become close friends with Reyes and his wife, Anne. The boys could have made more money, but instead they made a friend, which is far more important. True to our commitment to the fine wine business, we used the proceeds from the sale of the Samuel Adams franchise to make a move that would change the business forever.

During one of my frequent trips to the Napa Valley, I identified Silverado Vineyards and Schramsberg as excellent targets for national distributorship, but we couldn't entice either to join us: Silverado Vineyards' Jack Stuart was close with his marketer, and Schramsberg wanted to go it alone.

The agent for Silverado wanted to block our overtures, so to take us off track he told the president of Markham Winery, Bryan Del Bondio, that we were looking for another California property for our portfolio. Mercian, the Japanese food giant, had just purchased the winery for $13 million and spent another $8 million updating it. At the time Markham was selling only 20,000 cases a year, and Del Bondio realized that a $21 million investment for 20,000 cases was not going to cut it for Mercian. He needed to grow the sales fast, but unfortunately, he didn't have the sales organization to do it.

We were already acquainted with Del Bondio because Pacific was his Chicago distributor, so when Bill and I invited him to play golf, he warmly accepted. A week after that outing, we became the U.S. agents for Markham: We got what we wanted, and Del Bondio was in a much better position to justify Mercian's investment.

This relationship continued to bear fruit in the future. A few years later, we formed a joint venture with Mercian to produce a wine under the name Glass Mountain. Within five years, the combined sales of Markham and Glass Mountain surpassed 300,000 cases. Del Bondio was happy, Mercian was happy, and we were happy. Through the years, our personal friendship with Del Bondio has continued to grow, and we are pleased to continue to represent Markham to this day.

———————

Over time, both of my sons earned their leadership roles in our family business. Bill was named president of Paterno Wines International at age thirty-five, and John became president of Pacific Wine Company a year later. Their contributions, along with those of Scribner and Kournetas, allowed me to focus on new challenges.

One of these challenges, of course, was grandparenting. Before they were school aged, I began taking Bill's children to the Ravinia Music Festival in nearby Highland Park each summer to hear classical music. We would spread out a blanket on the grass and have a picnic on the lawn while the orchestra and soloists performed in the pavilion. By their tenth birthdays, they had all been to the Lyric Opera.

Once, little JoJo decided to discuss her adventure at the opera for show-and-tell. A classmate asked, "How can you stand to go to an opera?"

JoJo replied, "It's great. I get dressed up in a party dress and go to Everest for dinner with my grandmother and grandfather. Chef Joho cooks lobster for us, and then we go to the beautiful opera house where the people are all dressed up. We watch people in costumes sing—sometimes a lot of them at one time—and every once in a while everyone claps. A half hour later, we go home. We love it when Nanna and Nonno take us to the opera."

It took a while for my grandchildren to realize that we always left after the first act: We kept it short so they would want to go back again the next year. (Of course, Joho's lobster was a pretty good bribe, too.)

My grandparents and my parents had always emphasized the importance of family, but I was an only child. Having two sons of my own was an enlightening experience, and seeing the differences in their personalities and the ways they approached their work was a lesson in contrasts. Bill's business background enables him to visualize plans that he can quickly put into operation. John's methodical nature is bolstered by his strong fundamental business skills, and he is skilled at using metrics to increase productivity and efficiencies. John's talents and his law-school training ideally suit him to prepare our organization to accommodate the tremendous growth that's generated year after year by Bill and his team.

I always knew that both would complement me in our business, but it gives me such pleasure to know that the choice of working with me had been made by them alone.

Spirals alla Rustica

When pressed for time, this simple pasta dish with a tomato-basil sauce is the perfect comfort food. It proves that a bowl of pasta and a glass of wine is a wonderful way to end the day.

SERVES 5

⅓ cup extra-virgin olive oil

Pinch red pepper flakes

3 cloves garlic, ¼-inch dice

1 handful flat-leaf parsley, chopped

1 handful basil (10–15 leaves), chopped

12 fresh ripe plum, or San Marzano, tomatoes, coarsely chopped

Salt and pepper, to taste

1 pound spiral pasta

Ricotta Salada or Parmigiano-Reggiano cheese, freshly grated

1. Heat the olive oil, adding a pinch of red pepper flakes. Sauté the garlic, parsley, and basil in the oil. As soon as the garlic begins to brown, add the chopped tomatoes and stir. Season with salt and pepper and cook until tomatoes are done, about 12 to 15 minutes.

2. Salt and bring 6 cups of water to a boil; cook the spirals in the salted water. While the spirals are cooking, ladle about 5 tablespoons of the sauce into warm pasta bowls.

3. When the pasta is *al dente*, drain well. Ladle spirals over the sauce in the bowl, and then ladle about 5 tablespoons of sauce over the spirals and sprinkle liberally with cheese and freshly ground pepper. Serve at once.

Suggested Wines
Terlato Family Vineyards Syrah, Rutherford Hill Cabernet Sauvignon, Cuvaison Cabernet Sauvignon

LAMB LOIN IN A BREAD-CRUMB CRUST

There are a few things I always keep in the freezer if we need to entertain guests on short notice. Lamb loins are simply delicious prepared in a seasoned bread-crumb crust, sauced with mushrooms, and paired with a big red wine.

SERVES 4

1 lamb loin, whole

Olive oil

1 cup bread crumbs

½ cup Parmigiano-Reggiano cheese, grated

Salt and pepper, to taste

¼ cup parsley, finely chopped

2 cloves garlic, minced

¼ cup onion, minced

12 mushrooms, sliced

3 tablespoons butter

Red pepper flakes, to taste

3 ounces veal stock

1. Set broiler at 475°F. Rub loin with olive oil. Mix bread crumbs, cheese, salt, pepper, parsley, garlic, and onion.

2. Spread half of the bread crumbs on a sheet of aluminum foil large enough to accommodate the loin. Press loin down to coat. Spread remaining bread crumbs over top of loin and press down. Keep at room temperature 10 minutes or so. Then, press down again and place on a baking pan. Place pan in middle rack of oven.

3. Cook for 4 minutes or so. Turn loin over and cook 4 minutes or so for rare.

4. Remove from the oven and cover with aluminum foil for 5 minutes.

5. While the loin is cooking, in a skillet over medium heat, sauté the mushrooms in 2 tablespoons of butter. Sprinkle in red pepper flakes, salt, and pepper. Stir in remaining butter. Lower the heat to simmer.

6. Add the veal stock and continue stirring.

7. Cut the loin into 6 ½-inch slices. Place in a dish and fan slices. Spoon mushroom sauce over the meat and serve.

SUGGESTED WINES
Luke Donald Claret, Sokol Blosser Pinot Noir "Old Vineyard Block," Terlato Family Vineyards Devils' Peak

Old Stones and New Vines

MANAGEMENT IS DOING THINGS RIGHT; LEADERSHIP IS DOING THE RIGHT
THINGS.

—*Peter F. Drucker*

I WAS HAPPY ABOUT OUR DECISION IN 1987 TO MOVE TO Lake Forest to be closer to Bill and his family, and JoJo especially loved being close to her grandchildren. The long-established community on the North Shore of Chicago also provided ideal educational opportunities for Bill's growing family. But the twenty-five-mile drive into the city to our corporate headquarters in Chicago was getting increasingly difficult and time-consuming. We were outgrowing our buildings on Western Avenue, so we began to contemplate buying land and building a corporate headquarters somewhere west of the city, near O'Hare Airport.

Both problems were solved one Saturday morning in the fall of 1995. I was reading the local newspaper while drinking my morning coffee and spotted an eye-catching article—"Estate for Sale," the headline announced. The author made a point of saying, "Estates are never sold; the title is only transferred." I liked the sound of that.

The property in question was the Armour estate in Lake Bluff, designed in 1916 by the famous architect Harrie T. Lindeberg for the meatpacking heir Philip D. Armour III and his wife, Gwendolin.

According to the article, no matter who the new owner might be, the castle-like mansion called Tangley Oaks would always be referred to as the Armour estate.

Other Chicago business tycoons—Augustus Swift and Marshall Field, for example—chose to build their mansions on the shores of Lake Michigan in Lake Forest and an adjacent community, Lake Bluff. Instead, the Armour estate was built on 216 acres five miles west of the lake to ensure the privacy that the land between the village and the main railroad could provide. Sixteen years in planning and construction, the residence was finally completed in 1932. It is considered by many architects to be one of the finest examples of a Tudor Gothic residence in the United States. The best part? The Armour estate was only a five-minute drive from both Bill's home in Lake Forest and ours as well.

My son John came for dinner the evening I'd seen the ad, and I asked if he would make an appointment with a real estate agent so we could see the interior. I had no intention of purchasing it; I just wanted to see it. But as we drove into the long, tree-lined entrance, I experienced a very tranquil feeling. This was the closest thing I'd seen in the United States to the magnificent stone *palazzos* (palaces) and *castellos* (castles) of Milan, Venice, and Palermo and the châteaux in France that I'd seen.

We walked through the magnificent front entrance and toured the building for about an hour. I saw elaborate carved wooden doors and mantels, leaded glass windows, soaring columns, Tudor arches, marble fireplaces, linenfold paneling, torchères, chandeliers, and Marie Antoinette floors—doweled, not nailed. It was the perfect setting for us.

When we returned home, I suggested to John that Tangley Oaks could, and should, be the corporate headquarters for Paterno Wines International. We went back with Bill the next day, and afterward, we all agreed it was the right place for us. It was a reflection of how we felt about our business, which did not seem to fit well in a high-rise building. For me personally, walking through the Armour estate was like revisiting those centuries-old European castles that held mysteries at the end of every corridor and hosted endless feasts in every vaulted dining room.

I'm not much for bargaining. I told the real estate agent to quote me the price and I'd either buy it or walk away. There'd be no dickering, no up-and-down negotiating, and no nonsense. The next day, he called me with the price. It was fair, and I told him, "Sold!"

The following week, the title was transferred. As the writer said, "This estate will always be the Armour estate," but I live and breathe in it with great satisfaction every day. We had purchased a historical landmark. Although the Armours had subdivided the original property and sold parcels to developers, the mansion's grounds still boasted seven acres of land overlooking an idyllic pond.

In 1953, the Armour family sold the mansion and land to brothers Warren and Bob Davis, who housed their United Educators reference book firm there until 1995. The years had taken their toll, and Tangley Oaks needed to be restored to accommodate our needs. Knowing that we intended to restore the building to its original condition, the real estate agent advised us to contact Tom Rajkovich, an architect who was a Lindeberg expert and happened to live on the North Shore.

I called Rajkovich and asked if he would be interested in walking through the building with me. For hours, we toured the building, and I was impressed by his enthusiasm for and knowledge of Lindeberg's work. Afterward, I invited him to come to my home for dinner, and quickly phoned JoJo to begin boiling water for pasta. We had dinner, drank a bottle of 1990 Brunello di Montalcino Il Poggione, and talked until one in the morning.

I told him I needed him to work for me for a year. I couldn't tell him exactly what the terms would be, and I didn't know what salary he would expect, but I wanted him to oversee the work that would be needed to bring the estate back to its original state. Because I was essentially asking him for a year of his time, he told me he'd need to talk the offer over with his wife. A few days later, he called me and told me what he would need to leave his practice and join the project for a year. His request was very fair, and I didn't hesitate to say yes.

John's love of architecture was a tremendous asset for the renovations; he worked well with Rajkovich and accurately conveyed our vision of the mansion. In the end, the restoration took more than a year to complete. The building had no hot water, no air conditioning, and a deplorable heating system. The entire house had to be rewired. The roof had to be replaced, as well as most of the handcrafted lead gutters. The wood floors needed refinishing, and the sixteen-inch walls needed to be expertly repaired and repainted in colors approved by the National Historical Society. The leaded-glass windows were in need of repair, and it was difficult to find artisans to do that kind of work. None of the nine fireplaces was working, and all needed repair.

As gastronomy was an important part of our work, we had an urgent need for a proper commercial kitchen. The only useful thing in the mansion's existing kitchen was the walk-in safe that had been used to house the Armours' silver service.

Jean Joho had come to Chicago from his native Alsace to head up the kitchen in Maxim's de Paris, and then he moved on to become the chef-owner of the three-star Chicago restaurant Everest. He was outgoing, passionate about wine and food, and a great friend to me. He was also the logical choice to design a kitchen at Tangley Oaks. Not only did Joho design the kitchen—he also contacted all of the kitchen equipment purveyors and ordered everything on our behalf. He inspected the kitchen once a week during construction to make sure everything was installed properly, and he even did me the honor of preparing the dinner for the first large party we hosted at Tangley Oaks.

Rajkovich also brokered the restoration of some of the Armours' heirloom furnishings and rugs that had been sold to the Davises and placed in storage. Original wallpapers were either restored or reproduced, and every effort was made to furnish the first-floor living areas in a manner that was appropriate for the initial design of the home. The second floor of the building was devoted to offices for our senior managers; these offices all have lovely views of the pond and forests that surround the building. In all, the 26,000 square-foot mansion accommodates sixty-five employees and also provides ample space for entertaining.

Shortly thereafter, we bought another building in nearby Bannockburn to house our finance team, information-technology department, creative department, and management staff for one of our distribution companies. In a woodsy setting, the building provides space for more than sixty employees, with beautiful offices overlooking a pristine natural forest setting. Best of all, it's only a fifteen-minute drive from Tangley Oaks.

————

The year 1996 brought many changes. Not only did we move to Tangley Oaks and Bannockburn, but we also realized a dream I'd had for years: My sons and I purchased a winery in the Rutherford appellation of the Napa Valley. The appellation, which includes many of the historic mid-Valley vineyards—Beaulieu Vineyards, Robert Mondavi Winery, Niebaum-Coppola Estate Winery, and

Joseph Heitz Cellars—was originally part of George C. Yount's five-hundred-acre Rancho Caymus land grant. The soil is rocky and enriched by volcanic ash, and Yount's first grape stock was the first of a long succession of quality plantings.

In 1972, Bill Jaeger, Chuck Carpey, and other partners bought the former Souverain of Rutherford Winery, which Joseph Phelps had built four years earlier. They renamed it Rutherford Hill Winery, concentrated on Merlot as their trademark wine, and constructed 56,000 square feet of caves in the foothills of the Vaca Range to provide European-style barrel aging for thousands of barrels of wine. In the early 1980s, the brand reached nearly 100,000 cases per year in sales.

Unfortunately, around that same time, they made some marketing errors in an effort to boost sales. (At the time we purchased the winery, in 1996, their sales had dipped to around 65,000 cases per year.) Prior to the purchase, Bill Jaeger's son Jeff had approached Pacific Wine to become the winery's Illinois distributor. In 1993, we took over the brand's national distribution and put together a five-year plan for the facility, grape sources, and equipment. In two years, we built the brand up to 80,000 cases a year, and at that point, the Jaegers informed us that they planned to sell the winery.

Our long-term agreement with Rutherford Hill had about fifteen years remaining, which would, of course, have to be honored by the new owners. After a few months passed, we were advised that a sale was imminent. After discovering who the potential buyer was, I knew right away that we wouldn't be able to work with them because they had a reputation for quantity, rather than quality, wines. I was disappointed and asked Jeff Jaeger why he would sell to them, after we had worked so hard to turn his brand around. To his credit, Jaeger said, "If you want to buy the winery, just pay us what was offered, and we'll sell it to you."

It was a bolt out of the blue, and there were many things to consider. Rutherford Hill had been the first winery to focus on Merlot, way back in 1972, so it had its place in Napa history. Because of our hard work, the brand was finally on the upswing. We had known what was required to turn the brand around, but could we improve on this success as owners?

Bill and John were enthusiastic about the challenge, so we decided to find out. Bill and Scribner worked out the details with the Jaegers, and in the fall of 1996, we became the owners of Rutherford Hill Winery. It was a momentous occasion. It had been nearly fifty years since I began dreaming of being a winemaker while working in my father's store. Now, with my sons at my side, I was living that dream.

Unfortunately, many of the winery's responses to problems hadn't been solutions. Instead of making less wine and making it better, they'd chosen to make more wine, cheaper. We'd inherited a brand in quality decline. We realized that if we were going to make good wine, we were going to have to change the sources of our grapes and the entire vinification process. Another plus: The prime location of the winery, which shares an entrance road with the exclusive Auberge du Soleil resort, made it a great destination for wine tastings, picnics under olive trees, tours, and social events in the wine caves.

Fortunately, there were also some really good people working at Rutherford Hill. Willis Blakewell was the accountant, Kelly Holmes was secretary to Bill Jaeger, and Laryl Smith was the facility manager. The winery staff was supervised by Juan Marino, Sr., who had been there for more than twenty years.

We all connected from the start, and they knew exactly what I had in mind. We promoted Blakewell to general manager, and I asked Holmes to be my assistant. We worked together to improve every area of the winery, from the quality of the wine to the visitor experience to the appearance of the physical plant. You name it, we rebuilt it or redesigned it.

At the same time we were renovating and moving into Tangley Oaks, Blakewell oversaw the construction of a "winery within a winery" for reserve wines and experimentation at Rutherford Hill. Holmes began working on beautifying the grounds, including the picnic area that overlooked the Napa Valley, and updating the retail room. In the olive grove, Smith built a gazebo with spectacular views of the Napa Valley.

The mile-long caves were refurbished because we intended to use them for visitor tours and parties. We brought in Italian-made chandeliers, installed wrought iron sconces along some of the walls, and placed torchères at the entrance. The caves were already functional, but I wanted them to also reflect the spirit of quality that I believed should permeate the winery. I made it clear to my staff that it was their responsibility to make sure visitors to the Valley considered a visit to Rutherford Hill to be *the* most worthwhile part of their trip.

During my first week as owner, I met with the staff and distributed mock-ups of a cover of *Wine Spectator* magazine featuring a bottle of Rutherford Hill Merlot and a simple headline: "#1 Merlot in Napa Valley." The issue date was September 2002. I passed them out to the management team and simply said, "Look at the date in the corner. I'm giving you five years to get me there. I'm serious about this. What do you need to make this a reality?"

First, we cut annual production by 14,000 cases, which eliminated inferior lots before the final blend of the 1995 vintage. It was a very costly move, but I'd preached quality and had to prove I was serious about it. The 1996 vintage of our Merlot evolved into a wine with rich aromas of black cherry, plum, cedar, and black pepper. The turnaround was underway.

The final ingredient of the success of Rutherford Hill was the long-term contracts we signed with some of the best growers in Napa Valley. We'd conducted blind tastings of their wines before the final blending process. This allowed the winemaking team to select the best lots and blend them to achieve a consistent, enjoyable, and identifiable style.

Unfortunately, it takes about ten years for consumers to catch up with the changes a winery makes. After vines are planted, it takes a minimum of five years before the fruit can be used. The vines we planted in 1997 wouldn't be usable until the 2002/2003 vintage. Red wine needs a minimum of two years in the barrel and then some bottle age beyond that. Therefore, the first vintage over which we had total control would reach the consumer no sooner than 2005/2006—almost ten years after planting the vines. Ten years before the consumers, journalists, and wine critics discovered the work we'd done, we already knew how good our wines would be. It became more than a little frustrating to me to read ratings that had been written eight years before, knowing how much we had changed the wine.

We were able to make small changes that made a palpable difference in the meantime. We made a better wine in 1999/2000 by ceasing to do business with all of the growers who had been supplying the winery with inferior fruit through the mid 1990s. In 2000, we invited growers to blind tastings of barrel lots of Rutherford Hill wines. After they rated all the barrel lots, including those made from their own grapes, we'd approach the ones with the lower scores and tell them, "The wine you rated last was yours. I'm expecting better from you next year, or we'll cancel your contract." A number of them responded positively the next year. Some didn't, so we cancelled their contracts and began to farm much of the fruit ourselves.

Many years before, Bob Mondavi had predicted that I'd own a

winery some day. His words must have made more of an impression on me than I'd thought. After investing more than $7 million in the improvement and expansion of Rutherford Hill, I had a new appreciation for the phrase "capital-intensive," and I was beginning to understand the demands and idiosyncrasies of winemaking.

The acquisition of Rutherford Hill also signaled my initiation into the Napa Valley wine community. Since I felt it was necessary to spend time at the winery and become part of the community in the valley, I purchased a home in the hills east of St. Helena overlooking Meadowood Country Club.

In 1999, I began a new California tradition—an annual "Duck and Risotto Dinner" at our Napa home. Wine legend Dan Duckhorn prepares the duck, and I make the risotto, and many Napa Valley winemaking luminaries join us each year for the meal. The guests gather in the kitchen while we prepare the risotto, and Dan grills the duck on the barbeque he brings from home. We drink only French and Italian wines—usually Gaja and Chapoutier. Just to liven up the mix, I occasionally invite a celebrity: legendary jazz pianist Ramsey Lewis graced the table at one of the dinners.

By far the most anticipated event in the region is the annual Auction Napa Valley. Bidders compete with each other for luxury items, events, and bottles of rare and collectible wine, all to benefit several Napa Valley charities. During the 2000 auction weekend, Rutherford Hill Winery hosted its first Celebrity Chef Dinner, an elaborately staged formal party for fifty guests. The party was held in a large tent positioned outside the tasting room, with beautiful views of the Valley. Jean Joho was the first celebrity chef and my assistant, Kelly Holmes, handled the decor for the party. It was exquisite—red carpets, gold tablecloths, sparkling white china, crystal, and flowers everywhere.

The whole family was in attendance, and we began the evening with Champagne and hors d'oeuvres in the candlelit caves. Then, our guests moved into the tent, and the feast began as the sun set over the vineyards. After dinner, the guests moved to our tasting room patio for espresso, grappa, cigars, and music.

Joho helped organize future Celebrity Chef Dinners by tapping many of his chef friends—Hubert Keller of Fleur de Lys restaurant; Grant MacPherson, then the executive chef at the Bellagio; Pierre Schaedelin of Le Cirque; Michel Ricard of Citronelle in Washington, D.C.; Dean Fearing, who made his name at Dallas's Mansion at Turtle Creek and now has his own eponymous restaurant; and another longtime friend of mine, Piero Selvaggio of Valentino's in Santa Monica. One of the gala dinners at Rutherford Hill was prepared by our executive chef, Colin Crowley, who served a hot and delicious risotto course paired with the 1999 Rutherford Hill Chardonnay in the fifty-five degree wine caves. What a risk! What a cherished memory!

Although Rutherford Hill Winery received a lot of my attention during those heady years, our company had also begun to expand in some very interesting directions. We were already partnering with Chapoutier to produce a Rhône wine named Entré Nous. In 1998, Chapoutier traveled to Australia with Bill to search for vineyards and discovered prime vineyard soil on an eastern-facing slope on the southern edge of the Pyrenees wine region. He called me immediately, saying, "I have found a soil from which greatness is possible."

I matched Chapoutier's excitement, telling him we would be happy to market the wines he'd cultivate there in the United States. Chapoutier replied, "No, no, I'm calling because we should be partners in this venture. We must produce the wine together."

Outspoken, flamboyant, brilliant, and daring—these are some of the words that have been used to describe Michel Chapoutier, the young man I'd met years before in his father's vineyard. Without question, he is one of the world's greatest winemakers and one of the wine world's most fascinating personalities. Chapoutier is widely known as an innovative seventh-generation winemaker whose unique and meticulous methods of cultivation have become an authentic philosophy for his *domaine*.

As a young winemaker, Chapoutier's allegiance to the soil and reverence for *terroir* (soil) was sometimes startling to observers. He rejected chemicals, worked according to the lunar calendar, embraced biodynamic farming years before it became commonplace, used indigenous yeasts, and cast off "press wine"—all surprising departures from the usual business of winemaking. Chapoutier does everything and anything to encourage the voice of the vineyard to speak loudly in his wines, and his techniques require rigorous management and close attention to detail. This dedication to traditional winemaking methods gives his wines their unmatchable flavors, aromas, and excellence.

The result? In a single three-year period, Robert Parker awarded no fewer than five of Chapoutier's wines perfect 100-point scores.

With all this in mind, I responded, "Of course, Michel, it will be a pleasure to be your partner in wine production."

We purchased the land together, formed a joint venture, and planted one hundred acres of *vitis vinifera*. The first few years, we lost eighty-three acres to drought and frost, but the remaining seventeen acres produced Terlato & Chapoutier's inaugural vintage in 2004. Terlato & Chapoutier lieu dit Malakoff and a Shiraz-Viognier blend were the first wines produced by the partnership. Robert Parker rated a barrel sample of the first vintage 2004 of the

Shiraz lieu dit Malakoff a 92, remarking, "There is no question Michel Chapoutier remains one of the most compelling wine personalities in the world, and his obsession with *terroir*-based wines is largely unequaled by any other *vigneron* [vine grower] on Planet Earth." Not bad for the first wines from struggling young vines.

The vineyards are planted and cultivated according to sustainable vineyard principles and practices. They provide very low yields of one to one-and-a-half tons per acre. There was no sophomore slump following the tremendous reception to the wine's 2004 debut; the next vintage sold out entirely in response to Parker's 91 rating.

As we rapidly expanded into winemaking, we realized it was time to form a holding company. We named the company Terlato Wine Group and housed three divisions under it: national sales and marketing, wholesale sales and distribution, and wineries and brands. Because we'd been so successful with our Rutherford Hill venture, and we now had experience running a winery, we were ready to put our newfound expertise to greater use.

———————

At a 1999 wine tasting in Napa, John chatted with Vic Motto, cofounder and president of Global Wine Partners, a Napa Valley-based investment firm that specializes in wine industry mergers and acquisitions. Motto expressed a desire to do some business with us, and John expressed his desire to purchase an important winery. Almost immediately, Motto set up a meeting with Hack Wilson, the owner of Chimney Rock Winery. Chimney Rock is one of the jewels of Napa Valley, with 123 acres of prime Stags' Leap District soil.

Rutherford Hill had been an outright purchase, but Chimney

Rock would be more complicated. The Wilson family wanted to sell the winery because Hack was growing older and didn't want to run it much longer. In May 2000, Bill negotiated the purchase of a fifty percent interest in Chimney Rock Winery.

Wilson, who had been a hotelier and soft-drink marketer, was a close friend of Alexis Lichine. At one point, Lichine advised Wilson to purchase a Bordeaux château that had become available. Unfortunately, the deal fell through at the last moment; annoyed, Wilson turned to Napa Valley in 1980 and acquired the Chimney Rock property. He immediately began making Cabernet Sauvignon—with an eye to the Bordeaux style.

The Chimney Rock property included a golf course, which Wilson cut in half to plant more vines on the property. He believed he'd entered the business to make wine, and he was serious about the process. Wilson took an interest in every aspect of the winemaking process, even moving into a home on the hillside just above the winery.

Chimney Rock's hospitality center had been built in the seventeenth-century architectural style of Cape Dutch buildings, and the winery was designed in the South African Huguenot style. Set back from the Silverado Trial, Chimney Rock's chalky white exteriors and regal poplar trees framing the vineyard's buildings set a beautiful scene. At the time we negotiated the purchase, sixty acres had been planted with Cabernet Sauvignon, and the 1998 and 1999 vintages were not in the bottle yet.

Our agreement with Wilson was a partnership. We agreed to run the business together, and Wilson could continue in the business as long as he liked. It permitted him to do what he loved most for as long as he could, and it also provided an orderly transition: We would take complete control of the winery upon his death, or at any point that he decided he did not want to continue working.

Our purchase of Chimney Rock also allowed us to work with Doug Fletcher, who at the time was the respected winemaker of Chimney Rock's Cabernet Sauvignon. Within moments of meeting him, I asked Fletcher, "Can you make great wines?"

"Yes."

"What do you need?"

Eleven million dollars later, I found that he was a man of his word. The 1998 vintage he made for us was spectacular. In some tastings, Chimney Rock's 1998 received higher ratings than the 1997 vintages of many other area wineries—surprising, since 1997 was widely considered to be a better vintage. Unfortunately, some journalists trashed the entire 1998 vintage, so we had to work harder to get it to market.

In 1999, Fletcher delivered yet another glorious wine, and he hasn't missed yet. One of his secrets is something he calls the "balanced vine" principle. Fletcher strives to achieve balance between the length of the root system and the number of leaves on the vine, because doing so keeps the water supply at just the right level to moderately stress the vines. The result is a vine that produces smaller berries with intense varietal character.

The proof is in the bottle. The Cabernet Sauvignons that predated the introduction of balanced vines had a green olive character, and the wines made from balanced vines have intense black cherry and deep berry flavors more characteristic of Margaux. In 2002, we cemented our commitment to making these great wines by replanting the remaining sixty-three acres of the property with Cabernet Sauvignon.

In addition to making wine, we were also growing our import business. I had pursued Angelo Gaja for twenty-five years (a bit before wine writers had recognized his genius) about importing his outstanding wines. His response was always a very polite, "Perhaps someday." Twice a year, I sent him letters, just to make sure he would not forget us.

At the end of 2000, I received an e-mail from Gaja asking if I planned to attend Vinitaly, the annual Italian wine exposition in Milan. I hadn't planned to go—Bill would be attending—so I arranged for Gaja to meet with Bill instead. I knew he had to be planning a move, because Gaja is a very serious man who doesn't ask to meet unless he has something significant to discuss. I told Bill to be prepared.

Bill called the moment the meeting was over. "We have Gaja for the United States."

I immediately e-mailed Gaja, telling him, "I've waited twenty-five years for this day."

"Was it worth it?" he responded.

"Yes," I wrote back.

Many thought we should have had Gaja long before. In response, I'd say that twenty-five years ago, few people knew who Angelo Gaja was. Today, the entire world knows his wines, and he could choose any importer in the United States. He chose us, and it was well worth the wait.

———————

The January 2001 addition of Gaja wines to the Paterno portfolio marked the beginning of another important and fast-moving period of progress for the Terlato Wine Group. In early 2000, I asked Fletcher to create a wine that could challenge the other well-respected California Meritage Bordeaux blends. His challenge: make a wine that was sourced entirely from grapes grown on our properties. The result was a wonderful, full-bodied wine that could easily have been launched as the inaugural vintage. But before the bottling, Fletcher told me, "I can do better. I've learned a lot about our vineyards with this Meritage."

I was pleased with his response. The Meritage was an exciting wine, but if people were going to pay $175 a bottle, it had to be a $175 bottle of wine. Fletcher experimented further, and in 2001, he knew we had the right wine for an inaugural vintage. I named this rich, powerful, and elegant wine EPISODE, and we offered the first 400 six-bottle cases we produced only to people that we knew appreciated fine wines.

Our company had entered the twenty-first century with our sights set on continually improving the quality of our portfolio. Now, that portfolio proudly included Terlato-owned vineyards. The date on each vintage took on a much deeper meaning.

Risotto with Shrimp, Mussels, and Clams

As part of our effort to revitalize Rutherford Hill Winery, we invited a French producer of Chablis to work with us to develop a California Chardonnay using Chablis vinification methods. When I mentioned to the chef that I wanted to share the 1999 vintage with our Wine Auction guests, he suggested this seafood risotto, despite the difficulties of serving a hot risotto to a large group in a cave (see p. 231). The results were spectacular, and this risotto is very doable for a smaller dinner party of six.

Serves 6

12 Manila clams

12 mussels

4 tablespoons olive oil

1 small tomato, peeled and chopped

2 garlic cloves, minced, divided

10 medium-sized shrimp, shells removed

½ cup chopped parsley

5½ cups fish broth

½ cup dry white wine

1 cup broth reserved from cooking the clams and mussels

2 tablespoons unsalted butter

2 tablespoons olive oil

½ cup minced onion

1½ cups carnaroli rice

1. Scrub clams and mussels. In a covered pot filled with 1½ cups of water, place the scrubbed clams and mussels. Cover the pot; bring to a boil and then simmer for a few minutes.

2. Remove the clams and mussels from the liquid, but do not discard the liquid. Discard any shells that did not open. Remove meat from the shells. Strain the liquid through a cheesecloth and reserve.

3. Heat the oil in a skillet and add one clove of garlic. Stir in the tomato, shrimp, and mussels. Add salt and pepper. Stir for about 5 minutes, remove from heat, and set aside.

4. Combine the fish broth with the mussel and clam liquid in a large saucepan. Bring to a steady simmer.

5. In a large casserole dish, over moderate heat, heat the butter and olive oil. Add the onion and remaining garlic and sauté for about 2 minutes, being careful not to brown.

6. Add the rice and stir continuously with a wooden spoon, making sure all the grains are well coated. Add the wine and stir until it is completely absorbed.

7. Add the simmering broth ½ cup at a time, stirring until each application of broth is absorbed.

8. After cooking for approximately 18 minutes, the rice should be cooked. Add in the seafood and parsley. Stir vigorously about 2 minutes to combine all ingredients and serve immediately.

SUGGESTED WINES
Chimney Rock Fumé Blanc, Hanna Sauvignon Blanc, Wairau River Sauvignon Blanc

Celebrations, Golden and Otherwise

FIFTY YEARS AGO, I BEGAN MY CAREER WITH DUAL influences: Bob Mondavi's uniquely California perspective and the Eurocentric ideas of Alexis Lichine and Frank Schoonmaker. I became a Francophile and fell in love with the wines of Bordeaux and Burgundy. I had the good fortune of launching Sicilian Gold and Corvo Duca di Salaparuta, the first wine from Sicily to successfully penetrate the American market. Vittorio Gancia exposed me to a number of the great wines of Italy. Later, I found Santa Margherita Pinot Grigio, which is the best-selling imported wine over $19 a bottle in American history. In the 1980s and 1990s, my renewed interest in California wines catapulted me into winery ownership. And after all that, I truly believe this trip around the world of winemaking has just begun.

One evening, I visited a New York restaurant with an exclusively American wine list. I noticed eight or so Pinot Grigios on the list, and I asked the waiter how these American Pinot Grigios were selling.

He replied, "Very well—because of Santa Margherita, of course."

The waiter's response was food for thought. "We don't have a horse in that race," I thought to myself.

As soon as I returned to Chicago, I did what I usually do: research. I bought eight or nine American Pinot Grigios produced in California and Oregon and tasted them blind. To be brutally honest, none of them impressed me. I thought, "We should produce our own high-quality California Pinot Grigio, one that captures the true essence of the varietal."

I called Doug Fletcher to see if he believed he could find the fruit to make a high-quality Pinot Grigio in California. After a few months of searching, he called me back. "Well, I have good news and bad news. As you are aware, the Pinot Grigio grape is a distant cousin of Pinot Noir. It's from the same family. I found some land we might want to purchase for planting Pinot Grigio. That's the good news.

"Now, the bad news. The land is in the Russian River Valley. Do you really want to use that soil to plant Pinot Grigio that would sell for $24 a bottle when you could be planting Pinot Noir that would sell for $50 a bottle?"

I thought for a moment before responding. "I would like you to taste all the Pinot Grigios made in this country and let me know if you can make the best Pinot Grigio in America from that soil. If you say you can, the sacrifice is worthwhile. I know it is fiscally irresponsible, but I'll do it anyway."

Fletcher, who's never backed down from a challenge, ran with the idea. For the wine's 2003 vintage, we produced only 1,800 cases. As I'd hoped, this Pinot Grigio captured the freshness, the fruitiness, the balance of acidity, and the delightful cantaloupe and flower blossom aromas that are so strongly associated with Pinot Grigio.

We had the wine, but we struggled with the idea of the brand name. We set up a number of brainstorming sessions at our headquarters, and one day a young woman who had joined the company as an assistant brand manager for Santa Margherita offered the idea of Terlato Family Vineyards. I liked it immediately, but I asked her, "Why do *you* think that's the right name for this wine?"

She responded, "We have many brands. Rutherford Hill is known for Merlot. Chimney Rock is known for Cabernet Sauvignon. Sanford is well known for Pinot Noir. Alderbrook is known for Zinfandel and Syrah. Everyone knows you brought Pinot Grigio to America—you're considered the father of Pinot Grigio! It makes sense to use your name as the brand."

She'd sold me, but I thought it would be wise to consult Bill and John as well. After I saw their enthusiastic responses, Terlato Family Vineyards was born.

The next challenge was figuring out what image the Terlato Family brand should convey. Why was it born? What is its purpose? Eventually, I concluded that the mission of the Terlato Family Vineyards brand should be to produce wines from an appellation that is famous for a particular varietal. We had Pinot Grigio from the Russian River Valley, so the next step would be a Syrah from the Dry Creek Valley. After that, we could do Pinot Noirs from the Russian River Valley and the Santa Rita Hills. Down the road, my vision included a Chardonnay from Russian River and a Cabernet Sauvignon from Stags Leap. The brand was also perfect for our star Meritage, EPISODE, which we made from grapes grown in our own Napa Valley vineyards.

Throughout my career, I'd always visualized the role of a winery owner as similar to that of an opera composer or an artist. The wines you produce should reflect the person that you are. To reflect my beliefs about wine, the Terlato Family Vineyards should produce wines that are the best rendition of the best grapes from the best soil. We weren't looking to make high-alcohol blockbuster

wines. Our primary goal was to achieve a harmonious balance
in our wines—flavors, fruit, tannins, acidity, body, mouthfeel,
texture, and alcohol. I firmly believed that the tradition of quality
we had begun would persist well into the future.

Many years before, my father had told me, "A wine producer
can influence what the world drinks." As I pondered the future of
Terlato Family Vineyards, I realized that the potential was limitless.
Our company could produce great wines and be innovative as well,
perhaps even producing blends that had never been done before
in California. Why *shouldn't* we be the ones to revolutionize the
wine world? We knew what great wines tasted like, and we had the
desire, the passion and the resources to produce them.

With this in mind, I thought about what blends I wanted to
produce—what I would want to be identified with the Terlato
name. Immediately, I thought of paying homage to specific
viticultural areas by using the blends commonly associated with
that place. I have always loved the wines of the great châteaux of
Margaux, Pomerol, St. Émilion, and Pauillac. So the concept of
the Terlato Family Vineyards Peak wines was born: they would be
wines from viticultural areas known for the traditional blend of
varietals that made them famous.

In early June 2001, Rutherford Hill's viticulturist, Rob
Weinstock, joined Blakewell, Fletcher, and me for a drive up
to a six-and-a-half-acre vineyard perched on one of the hills on
Rutherford Hill Winery's southern flank. After scrutinizing the
earth, Weinstock said, "God made this soil to plant Cabernet
Sauvignon."

So we planted the Cabernet, and we named the wine that sprang
from those grapes Angels' Peak. Our commitment was costly, of
course: It cost more than $150,000 an acre to prepare the site and
plant the vines, but it was a worthwhile investment. That six-and-

a-half acres promised to yield the equivalent of about 1,500 cases of some of the best Cabernet Sauvignon in the valley.

Angels' Peak is a place that's very difficult to leave. The hill provides a one-hundred-and-eighty-degree view of the Rutherford Bench, with the Napa River weaving a silver line through the vineyards that border the two main highways leading from Carneros to St. Helena. Vines are planted as far as the eye can see on the land that was once home to the Native American tribe of the Wappo, who ate grapes from the wild vines that wound around the native trees of the valley.

———————

On that particular day, I had a very good reason to feel a connection with the land. Maintaining homes in Napa, Lake Geneva, and Lake Forest had conditioned me to live in harmony with the seasons. The wineries and the land we cultivated were increasingly becoming my focus, as my sons were deeply involved in the day-to-day operation of our importing, distributing, and marketing companies.

In 2002, Bill and John continued our worldwide expansion, extending our portfolio to include wines from New Zealand, Argentina, and Spain. At the same time, we expanded the depth of our California agency brands with the addition of Hanna. Later, we also reached an agreement to distribute the Oregon wines of Argyle and Sokol Blosser.

We also purchased an interest in Sonoma's Alderbrook Winery. Immediately after the acquisition, we had to spend more than $5 million to upgrade equipment and replant many of the vineyards, but the winery struggled to move the high inventories that had accumulated prior to our involvement.

To compound matters, we made a tactical error by closing

out the old inventory at low prices. When our vastly improved wine was released at the right price for a wine of its quality (of course, considerably higher than the closeout prices of the previous vintages) consumers were reluctant to spend more than they'd spent before. It took a significant amount of time to prove that our new wines were worth their price.

I learned a valuable lesson at Alderbrook. It is wiser to destroy excess inventory if it is inferior in order to maintain the integrity of the brand.

In 2004, we assumed full ownership of Chimney Rock. Always ready to lay down a new challenge for Doug Fletcher, I asked him to create a Sauvignon Blanc in the style of Château Haut-Brion Blanc. Of course, he accepted the challenge, and we created an innovative new white blend modeled after a great white wine of Bordeaux: Chimney Rock Elevage Blanc, a handcrafted, limited-production (300 cases) blend of Sauvignon Blanc and Sauvignon Gris.

We were juggling a rapidly expanding import and marketing business, six distributorships, four wineries, and three partnerships. When Bill first approached me about selling our distributorships, I told him it was unthinkable. He was respectfully persistent, eventually convincing me that we should put more of our resources into agency brands and managing and developing our wineries. After much deliberation, I painfully accepted the strategic decision to sell all six of our Illinois distributorships.

Although I knew it was the best way to go, the decision was a very difficult one. Over the span of fifty years, with a lot of hard work from many talented people, we had grown a two-man wine-bottling distributorship into a regional empire considered by many to have the most prestigious portfolio of fine wines in America. We were the largest wine-only distributor in the United States. But I had to face the fact that there were increasing uncertainties about how wines would reach the hands of consumers, particularly now that more and more wine was being ordered online, and new laws permitting direct winery sales were dramatically changing the landscape for distributors. If we didn't have the desire to expand our distributorships to other states, it was best for us to concentrate on the work Paterno Imports was doing. It also gave me more time and resources to concentrate on my newfound love—producing wine. Selling the distributorships meant an infusion of capital to invest in the future.

John had been president of the distributorships, so after the sale, he joined us at Tangley Oaks. John and his wife, Diana, and newborn son, Jack, moved from downtown Chicago to Lake Forest about a year and a half later. His new focus at Tangley Oaks was to expand the international sales operation to export wines from our agency brands and family-owned brands. In 2002, Paterno Imports became Paterno Wines International, a name that better reflected the structure of the business and our long-standing commitment to build our portfolio in the same way fine restaurants craft their wine lists—by balancing variety, region, style, and price.

Next, we focused on expanding our worldwide collection. In 2005, Bill negotiated an exclusive agency agreement to market Bollinger Champagne, Langlois-Château, and the illustrious Chanson Burgundies. The next year, we added Château des Laurets, a classic right-bank Bordeaux, and forged a relationship with the legendary Rothschild family.

Nothing can be more fortuitous or rewarding than meeting

people with the same interests. My sons and I are consistently attracted to individuals who share our passion for wine and believe quality is paramount. Bill encountered golf legend Ernie Els and South African winemaker Jean Engelbrecht, partners in a wine venture, at a golf tournament in Scotland. He was immediately impressed with the duo's long-term approach to the wine business.

Wine growing arrived in South Africa in the middle of the seventeenth century, courtesy of the Dutch East India Company. The winery Rust en Vrede was established not long afterwards, in 1694. Blessed with perfect weather, the South African soil produced a healthy volume of wine, but geographical, cultural, and political isolation caused the Rust en Vrede vineyard to fall into disrepair.

Things changed when Jannie Engelbrecht purchased the winery in 1977, and the Rust en Vrede estate was reborn. Rust en Vrede became the first private winery in the country to specialize in the exclusive production of red wines, and in the early 1980s, it became the first producer in South Africa to make a blend of Cabernet Sauvignon, Shiraz, and Merlot, an award-winning wine that became known as Rust en Vrede Estate.

In 1998, Engelbrecht handed the reins of Rust en Vrede over to his son, Jean. Shortly after assuming control, the younger Engelbrecht appointed Louis Strydom as head winemaker. Together, they worked to accelerate the evolution of Rust en Vrede's wines and image, making it more relevant on the international wine stage and enabling it to compete with the leading wines of the world.

Els became a part of the Rust en Vrede tradition when he formed a partnership with Jean Engelbrecht in 1999. The two had been good friends for many years, and both were committed to making great wine. The goal of the partnership of Engelbrecht and Els was to create superior South African red wines that could compete on the international stage. Both made a significant investment in the vineyards and wineries, and they remained personally involved in the decisions and development of the company, involvement that is clearly evident in the quality of their wines. Adding Engelbrecht Els wines, which include the brands Engelbrecht Els, Ernie Els, Guardian Peak, Cirrus, and Rust en Vrede, to our portfolio expanded our reach to the tip of the African continent.

Golf led to another fortuitous meeting in 2000. Bill met golf prodigy Luke Donald, then a student at Northwestern University, while he was taking golf lessons from Donald's coach, Pat Goss. Goss was inspired to get the two together because of their shared interests in wine, food, and sports cars and their shared competitive natures. Bill immediately liked the soft-spoken Donald, who he found to be respectful and mature beyond his years.

In the years since Bill and Donald met, Donald has had a dazzling career in golf. They have become close friends and play golf often; one afternoon on the links, they discussed the idea of producing a wine under the Luke Donald brand name.

Bill wasn't just interested in a celebrity endorsement. He wanted Donald, who knows his wine, to be involved in choosing the Bordeaux blend with him, so the two men visited Doug Fletcher and the winemaking team at the Rutherford Hill Winery. Fletcher created six various claret-style red Bordeaux blends harvested from the 2005 vintage. Luke and Bill tasted the final blends, and Luke's selection, a blend of forty-four percent Cabernet Sauvignon, forty-three percent Merlot, twelve percent Cabernet Franc, and one percent Petit Verdot, became the Luke Donald Claret 2005, which launched in 2008. Donald's personal involvement in the blending sessions in Napa ensures that the wines reflect his own personality and style.

As appreciation for the wines of Australia grows, so does our Australian collection. In 2006, Bill added a three-tiered collection from Two Hands Wines. Founded in 1999 by Adelaide entrepreneurs Michael Twelftree and Richard Mintz, Two Hands has been praised by Robert Parker as "the finest *négociant* operation south of the equator." Their wines showcase the best of Australia's most prized growing regions, with a focus on Shiraz from the Barossa Valley.

We have also extended our portfolio to Canada, adding Ice Wines from the noted Peller Estates. The care with which these wines are made produces a rare combination of sweetness and acidity, yielding wines that can be served mixed with Champagne as an aperitif and are very compatible with desserts. We are proud to add this unique selection to our portfolio.

In late 2007, we purchased the iconic Sanford and Benedict Vineyard. In a June 2005 *Wine Enthusiast* article titled "California's Best Single Vineyards," Steve Heimoff identified five properties—one of which was Sanford and Benedict —and wrote, "Buying wines from these five properties is as close to a guarantee of quality as you are ever going to get." The vineyard's sixty-eight acres of Pinot Noir and fifty-two acres of Chardonnay produce wines that are Burgundian in nature.

When I was still only considering the purchase, I told Doug Fletcher that he should expect another challenge. "If we prevail in owning this vineyard, I don't want us to make just another Pinot Noir and Chardonnay, I want to make a Chambertin and a Corton Charlemagne. I believe in this soil we can accomplish that."

After the purchase was complete, Fletcher toured the vineyard and called me with his verdict. "In this prized vineyard, we can produce the Chambertin of California." The Francophile in me was resurrected.

With an increasingly varied selection of our own wines and a unique portfolio of international wines, the kitchen and dining room at Tangley Oaks assumed much greater importance than the one at our facility at 2701 Western Avenue in Chicago. The spacious professional kitchen is up for any task. Our chef, Colin Crowley, creates lunches there every day for industry visitors, and he handcrafts exciting menus for numerous wine-related events.

After the move to Tangley Oaks in 1996, the kitchen became my laboratory. Crowley and I compose menus, test recipes, and carefully select ingredients. For example, every year our kitchen uses about 300 cases of canned Italian plum tomatoes, in addition to the fresh Roma tomatoes we purchase when they are in season. The current year's canned tomatoes become available each fall, so after their release, we purchase fifteen to twenty different brands for a "tomato tasting."

We begin by lining up twenty large white plates on the dining room table. A sample of each can goes onto each plate. Those that contain too much water, as well as those that are green and stringy, are discarded immediately. At that point, only three or four brands usually remain, and Crowley makes a tomato sauce using each brand. After comparing the sauces, we select a brand and purchase the entire amount we will need for the year. That way, our sauces remain consistent. We perform the same ritual when we select olive oil, balsamic vinegar, pasta, Parmigiano-Reggiano cheese, espresso, and even meats.

Naturally, the surroundings at Tangley Oaks help drive home the message of "dining well" as a lifestyle choice. The ambience of the dining room, with its eighteen-foot sculpted ceiling, mullioned windows, heirloom Persian carpets, torchères, sconces, and restored furniture, lend elegance to every meal.

To balance the formality of the dining room, we often kick off our lunches in the kitchen with a glass of Champagne and an *amuse bouche* (a little morsel) as Bill or John put the finishing touches on a pot of risotto. Often, our guests carry on the tradition of participating in the meal's preparation. Once we gather in the dining room, members of the staff serve a simple three-course meal, with a pasta or risotto course and white wine to start followed by an entrée selected to pair well with one of our red wines. The last course is generally a salad and coffee.

———————

I am very grateful that I still love my work. Many people don't. I consider myself even more fortunate that both of our sons enjoy working in our family-owned business with me.

My sons and I are also very lucky to have tolerant wives. JoJo and both of my daughters-in-law, Debbie and Diana, understand the demanding nature of our business. We travel often, and these trips are all business—we never mix work with vacation. We often try to make up for our frequent absences by taking short trips with friends and family to warm places—especially places where excellent golf, fly-fishing, food, and wine are easy to find.

Over the years, the need to get away for short breaks became more important to me. During the years of our corporate expansion in particular, our home in Lake Forest became an extension of our place of business, so JoJo and I escaped to our home in Lake Geneva on the weekends to relax by water skiing, golfing, and cooking for family and friends.

Because many of our friends had already acquired winter homes in the desert, we purchased a home of our own at the Vintage Club in Indian Wells, just a short drive from Palm Springs. The

golf and entertaining that we enjoyed in Illinois now carried over
to California. The Vintage Club is a retreat where we can play
golf, see friends every day, and share meals prepared by the club's
superb Alsatian chef, Alain Redelsperger. The club's wine program
was cited by *Travel & Leisure Golf* magazine as one of the top six
among private clubs in the United States, a tribute to Al Castro,
the clubhouse manager.

Of all the sports I've ever played, golf has certainly been the
most enduring and enjoyable. It has also been the most humiliating,
because it is so difficult to master. However, my game is much
better today because of Tony Manzoni, a golf pro who coaches at
the College of the Desert in Palm Springs.

Manzoni and I became good friends because we have so many
common interests—golf, Italian food, opera, fast cars, and, of
course, good wine. We watch pro golfer Ben Hogan's tapes for
hours to study where his hands, hip, kneecap, foot, head, and
shoulder are as he strokes the ball. After dissecting the tapes, we
hit the course for hours trying to emulate Hogan's style.

As I ease away from the everyday operations of our importing
company and concentrate on the business of winemaking, I am
finding more time to spend with friends who share many interests
with JoJo and me. Our friends enjoy wine and food, and it's always
our pleasure to make sure we've got something interesting to drink
and eat.

Most of our desert friends return to cooler climes for the summer,
as we do, and many of us visit each other over long weekends,
always making time for some golf and dinners. Sometimes, we'll
travel with a few other couples to Las Vegas for a few days to
visit our chef friends' restaurants—Jean Joho at the Paris, Paul
Bartolotta at Wynn, and Piero Salvaggio at the Venetian. (I don't
care for gambling, so golf and three well-prepared meals are the
way to spend time in Vegas for me.)

In 2002, we joined friends for a vacation in Sardinia and fell in love with the beautiful island. That trip was JoJo's inspiration for the pitch-perfect way to celebrate our fiftieth wedding anniversary: not with a catered event at a hotel, but with a family trip to the Sardinian hotel Cala di Volpe. The luxurious resort, developed by the Aga Khan on the unspoiled Costa Smeralda, was modeled after an old-fashioned Mediterranean fishing village, with archways, terraces, and towers that blended into the rocky countryside. It offered comfortable rooms, many dining options, tennis, swimming in the sea or in a saltwater pool, boating, and, of course, golf.

The trip provided a way to be with our sons and their families for ten uninterrupted days. JoJo and I flew to Rome with John, Diana, and their sons, Jack and Cutler, and from there we went on to Sardinia in a small plane. Bill and Debbie and their daughters, JoJo and Elise, stopped first in France to pick up their son, Tony, who had been working at Chapoutier's winery. We all arrived at Cala di Volpe the same day, and JoJo and I spent our fiftieth anniversary laughing, talking, eating, and drinking wine with the people we love best.

———————

As a family, we gather together often because we live so close to each other. The centers of our homes are the kitchens, where everyone congregates to talk and eat. When the grandchildren come over, everyone's in the kitchen: JoJo and I cook, and all the grandchildren get involved. Our eighteen-year-old grandson Tony enjoys making certain recipes of his own creation. John's son Jack has been chopping garlic, parsley, and basil since the age of four; his younger brother, Cutler, loves to stir the sauce.

Jack, Cutler, and I have initiated another tradition: "boys' night out." We visit a local sushi restaurant, and the boys tear through plates of shrimp, teriyaki chicken, and tuna carpaccio. Afterward, the boys have a sleepover at our home, and we all prepare and eat breakfast together the next morning. Time with my grandchildren is like heaven on earth, and of course JoJo enjoys visiting her daughters-in-law and especially loves spending time with John's youngest, Margaret Katherine, born in 2007.

My father-in-law has been gone now more than thirty years, but the company he built lives on, now under a new name. In 2007, John and Bill decided it was time to change the name of our company to Terlato Wines International, and JoJo agreed.

As vintners, we are realizing a vision that began a decade earlier, with the 1996 purchase of Rutherford Hill Winery. We now produce our very own great wines. At the same time, we continue to have the pleasure to market many of the finest wines in the world. We consider ourselves fortunate that the press continues to warmly acknowledge the wines of our portfolio.

Our partnership with Michel Chapoutier, in the Australian Pyrenees of western Victoria, continues to thrive, with all three vintages receiving critical acclaim from Robert Parker and Harvey Steinman in the *Wine Spectator*.

And my role continues to change. In the fall of 2006, we conducted a series of double-blind tastings at Tangley Oaks. One of the blind tastings was designed to benchmark the ranking of our EPISODE and Angels' Peak wines against with other world-class wines. After the tasting proved that our wines could share a table with the most iconic wines of the time, our executive team decided that we needed to spread this powerful message to the market. We decided that I would become a salesman again and return to the marketplace to promote our wines.

We've come a long way from 1947, the year my father-in-law became the owner of the Pacific Wine Company. Back then, if a restaurant offered wine, it was probably just called a red or a white, and it wouldn't set you back more than fifty cents a glass. Today, it's commonplace for restaurants to offer winemakers' dinners with elaborate tasting menus and pairings for each course. Wine cellars have become a big business. Wine auctions are highly publicized and attended. Wine enthusiasts visit wineries to taste wines, and many buy them by the case while they're there. *The Wine Advocate*, *The Wine Spectator*, *Wine Enthusiast*, *Wine & Spirits*, Stephen Tanzer's *International Wine Cellar*, and Paul Pacult's *The Spirit Journal* have done a lot to educate wine consumers. The Napa and Sonoma valleys are now top vacation destinations and very different from the places I visited more than fifty years ago on my honeymoon.

Although I do think wine has finally become part of the mainstream, I realize that we are just at the threshold of wine appreciation and its role in culture, society, and gastronomy. Today, more people than ever before can speak intelligently about wine. Guests expect to be served wine with dinner, and they expect that the wine will complement the dishes being served. In coming years, people will embrace wine like never before, and its connection with success, hospitality, and good taste will be burnished forever.

Playing a wide variety of roles in this wonderful industry— retailer, distributor, importer, marketer, vineyard owner, wine producer, and witness to this country's wine renaissance—has been an immense pleasure. To know that I have contributed to this renaissance in a small way by marketing and making great wines is a tremendous point of pride. Our sons are following in my footsteps, which pleases me tremendously. I fervently hope that our grandchildren will follow in their fathers' footsteps as well, and I want our boys to experience the joy of working with their children, too. I hope that their generation, and the generations after them, will always celebrate their holidays, weddings, anniversaries, and all other memorable moments with the fruits of the Terlato collection. Wine is my gift to them. It is from the soil. It is life-enhancing, delicious, and a wonderful blend of God's gifts and man's ingenuity. It is magic in the glass.

LAMB LOIN À LA BORDELAISE

It is always a pleasure for us to gather with our extended family—children and grandchildren—celebrating life's milestones, laughing, and enjoying well-prepared meals like this delicious lamb. Buon appetito!

SERVES 4

½ pound mushroom caps, sliced ¼-inch thick
2 tablespoons butter, divided
2 tablespoons olive oil, divided
2 cups espagnole sauce
1½ tablespoons tomato paste
1 clove garlic, crushed
1 lamb loin
1½ pounds potatoes, cut into small cubes
Salt and red pepper flakes, to taste
Chopped parsley, for garnish

1. Preheat oven to 325°F.

2. In a saucepan, brown the mushrooms lightly in 1 tablespoon each butter and olive oil.

3. Add espagnole sauce, tomato paste, and garlic to the saucepan and simmer for 5 minutes. Remove from heat, cover, and set aside.

4. Put remaining 1 tablespoon each butter and olive oil in a casserole dish and brown the lamb on medium-high heat. Add the mushrooms and potatoes and season with salt and red pepper.

5. Bake in the oven uncovered for 30 minutes. Raise the heat to 350°F and pour the espagnole mixture over the meat. Cook 29

minutes longer, basting continuously, until done. Turn off the oven and let lamb stand for 5 minutes.

6. Sprinkle with parsley and serve in the casserole dish.

Suggested Wine
EPISODE

Acknowledgments

MY LIFE HAS BEEN ENRICHED BY THE FRIENDSHIPS of countless people to whom I owe many thanks. Words cannot express my respect and love for JoJo, my wife of more than fifty years, and my admiration for my sons, Bill and John; my daughters-in-law, Debbie and Diana; and my grandchildren—JoJo, Tony, Elise, Jack, Cutler, and Margaret Katherine—who will carry on the Terlato name. It is my hope that the grapes that are being grown and harvested in the Terlato vineyards today will always remind them of their inheritance from the soil. It is my gift to them.

John Kournetas and John Scribner have been with me as Pacific Wine and Paterno Imports evolved into Paterno Wines International and, today, the Terlato Wine Group. These fine men, along with the long succession of faithful and loyal employees who have worked alongside me for many years, are a source of great happiness to me.

The members of the wine community with whom I have had business and personal relationships are too numerous to mention, but Robert Mondavi, Alexis Lichine, Vittorio Gancia, Angelo Gaja, and Michel Chapoutier have been there for me in a special way, providing inspiration, camaraderie, expertise, and partnership at crucial moments along the way.

In writing and publishing this book, I have had the help of a number of people, including our talented artistic director Todd Everett, Susan Holmer, and my assistant, Carolyn Turnmire. There are others who have made this book a reality, and I sincerely thank them for their patience and professionalism.

Over the years, my admiration has grown immensely for those in the culinary arts, vintners, my business associates, some competitors, and my colleagues, present and past; and, as the richness of life is measured in friends, I am fortunate to have numerous friends. We eat together, enjoy wines together, and enjoy life together sharing the same passion.

Finally, I dedicate this book to the generations that came before me: my father and mother, my grandparents, and my father-in-law. As I grow older, my appreciation for their love, sacrifice, and encouragement only grows deeper. There simply are no adequate words to convey my gratitude, but I hope this book takes a step in that direction.

—*Anthony J. Terlato*

Thank you all for your help and confidence.

Sonja and Bob Abate, Nick Alexos, Linda and John Anderson, Piero Antinori, Charaine and Peter Argentine, Oliver Arnold, Julie and Tubby Bacon, Chef Mark Baker, Chef Paul Bartolotta, Dan Berger, Kim Beto, Fabrizio Bindocci, Harold Binstein, Michael Binstein, Shoppy Binstein, Etienne Bizot, Tom Black, Didier Bloch, Anthony Dias Blue, Susan Sokol Blosser,

Jon Bonne, Niki and Constantine Boutari, Barbara and Alex Bowie, Daphne and Michael Broadbent, Jean and Cam Brown, Sally and Allan Bulley, Rosemarie and Dean Buntrock, Carri Calhoun, Monica and Lou Canellis, Tawny Cannata, Al Capitanini, Rhonda and Don Carano, Dave Carini, Don Carter, Jessie Casanova, Joe Castrilli, Jean-Michel Cazes, Dr. Leonard Cerullo, Belinda Chang, Harvey Chaplin, Wayne Chaplin, Jim Cheeley, Greg Christoff, Ruth Ellen Church, Carlyse and Art Ciocca, Dr. Larry Cone, Will Conniff, Roy Coppola, Tony Cosentino, Bill Cosmos, Gilles de Courcel, Kari and Dr. Anthony Daddono, Maggie and Mayor Richard M. Daley, Fred Dame, Barbara and Jack Daniels, Peter Danko, Bryan Del Bondio, Kimberly Delsing and Dick Vandersande, Marino DeMeo, Randall Denman, Bernard Dervieux, Arjun Dewan, Joe Dibetta, Marty and Rich Diodati, Dave Dobson, Robin and Ric Donnelley, Connie and Bill Dore, Alan Dreeben, Dan Duckhorn, Gary Enloe, Dr. Carl Eybel, Barbara Fairchild, Steve Fennell, Sam Ferraro, Kelly and Paul Fleming, Bob Foley, Jennifer and George Forbeck, Paul Franson, Jacqueline Fried, Giovanni Galati, Suzanne and Frank Gallo, Mike Garozzo, Peter Gasbarra, Ann and Mayor Ray Geraci, Mirofora and Dr. Anthony Geroulis, Douglas Giachino, Franco Giacosa, Vic Gianotti, Jeannine and Dick Giesen, Adi Giovanetti, Charlie Gitto, Nicole Glenn, Craig Goldwyn, Josh Greene, Dr. Barry Hackshaw, Ann and Bert Hand, Chris Hanna, Sparky and Jane Hauck, Nikki Hauser, Carol and Andy Hayes, Eleanor and Ray Heald, Carole and Dr. Leo Henikoff, Dr. Joel Hirschberg, Bondy and Tom

Hodgkins, Valeria and Agustin Huneeus, Rob Hunter, Jim James, Laura Jensen, Cynthia and Chef J. Joho, Ed Jonna, Sandra and Tom Jordan, C. J. Kang, Nick Kapsaskis, John Keller, Dorota Kenar, Lisa and Robert Kessler, Michel Lama, David Lane, Sue and Larry Larkin, Toni and Cory Lazzaroni, Franco Lenzini, Suzy and Mike Leprino, Richard Leventhal, Larry Levy, Jan and Ramsey Lewis, Melissa Linehan, Maurizio LoBosco, Sofia and Magistrato Gaetano LoCoco, Dr. Tom Lombardo, Connie and Bob Lurie, Count Alexandre de Lur-Saluces, Bob Luse, Tony Magliocco, Kay Malaske, Alan Mannason, Cathy and Tony Mantuano, Mario Marfia, Grace and Norman Mark, Todd Marsh, Mary Marshall, Carmine Martignetti, Mary Ann and Tony Martino, Luca Marzotto, Count Paolo Marzotto, Chef Livio Massignani, Dominic Mattucci, Meredith May, Larry Mayenschein, Stuart McCall, Earle McCutcheon, Jim McGuire, Ed Melia, Charles Merinoff, Jean Meyer, Chris Miller, Marco Minasso, Richard Mintz, Fedele Miranda, Steve Mocogni, Vincent Monaco, Joey Mondelli, Fiona Morrison, Vic Motto, Christian Moueix, Marc Mueller, Lee Murphy, Linda Murphy, Matt Murphy, Joan and Bubba Nelson, Debbie and Carlos Nieto, Giannola Nonino, Kathy and Tony Novelly, Len Nowicki, Roma Obracaj, Dena and Cos Occhipinti, Tony Orlando, Richard Ortiz, Michelle Pae, Potter Palmer, Frank Panicali, Bryan Parker, Homi Patel, Paul Pacult, Kelly Peterson-Holmes, Marylena and Carlo Pisano, Ed Pitlik, Mark Pope, Jackie and Ed Rabin, Michael Ragg, Drs. Ruth and Michael Ramsey, Joe Rance, Dave Razzano, Pamela Reardon, Francesco

Ricasoli, Jill and Bill Rice, John Richman, Karen and Bob Rishwain, Ezio Rivella, Norm Roby, Joe Rochioli, Tom Rochioli, Fred Rosen, Phil Rozen, Silvio Ruffino, Victor Salafatinos, Bruce Sanderson, Carol and Jack Sandner, Dr. Gary Schaffel, Jay Schuppert, Dave Scott, Patti Crutchfield Scribner, Ron Sedia, Hazel and Marvin Shanken, Ted Simpkins, Alpana Singh, Sue and Jackson Smart, Joe Spellman, Tom Steffanci, Harvey Steiman, Adam Strum, Mary Anne Sullivan, Sushi Kushi Toyo, Tadeo Suzuki, Louis Szathmary, Matt Szura, Stephen Tanzer, Marisa Taylor-Huffaker, the Terlato Family, Jack Thennes, Chef Rick Tramonto, Bob Tremain, Henry Trione, Michele Truchard, Irene Tuntas, Michael Twelftree, John Van Alphen, Annette and Peter Van Dyck, Brad Vassar, Michele Velting, Elizabeth Vianna, Chef Gabriel Viti, Jana Wacker, Chef Leo Waldmeier, Bruce Wallin, Charlie Wegener, Nancy and Dr. Lowell Weil, Sr., Rob Weinstock, Bruce White, Katherine White, Rob Whitley, Louise and Hans Willimann, Natalie Witty, Colleen Aloisio Wytmar, and Maurizio Zanella.

Recipe Key

Nonna Giarrusso's Veal and Melrose Peppers 34

Chicken alla Milanese 36

Cannoli 46

Paterno's Pan Pizza 64

Florentine Ravioli 66

Fettuccine with Shaved White Truffles 76

Saffron Bow Ties 77

Tournedos Rossini 86

Penne with Cognac 104

Steak with Mustard-Cognac Sauce 106

Chive Risotto with Truffle Oil 120

Filet Mignon Diane 122

Sautéed Clams 166

Toasted Ravioli 167

Linguine with Lobster Sauce 183

Penne St. Martin 199

Spirals alla Rustica 216

Lamb Loin in a Bread-Crumb Crust 218

Risotto with Shrimp, Mussels, and Clams 238

Lamb Loin à la Bordelaise 258